AVERTING
CATASTROPHE

AVERTING CATASTROPHE

STRATEGIES FOR REGULATING RISKY TECHNOLOGIES

Joseph G. Morone and
Edward J. Woodhouse

UNIVERSITY OF CALIFORNIA PRESS

Berkeley   Los Angeles   London

University of California Press
Berkeley and Los Angeles, California

University of California Press, Ltd.
London, England

© 1986 by
The Regents of the University of California

Library of Congress Cataloging-in-Publication Data

Morone, Joseph G.
  Averting catastrophe.
  Bibliography: p.
  Includes index.
  1. Technology assessment. 2. Risk. 3. Environmental
protection. I. Woodhouse, Edward J. II. Title.
T174.5.M68 1986   304.2'8 85-24607
ISBN 0-520-05723-6 (alk. paper)
ISBN 0-520-05754-6 (pbk.)

Printed in the United States of America

1 2 3 4 5 6 7 8 9

Contents

Preface

This volume attacks an intriguing puzzle: Why, despite close calls, have risky civilian technologies produced no catastrophes in the United States? Such technologies as toxic chemicals and nuclear power pervade contemporary life, and dire and sometimes compelling warnings of their hazards are as familiar as the silhouette of the Three Mile Island cooling towers. Yet so far, we have been free of major disaster. Have we simply been lucky—or is our good fortune at least partly the result of deliberate efforts to protect against these hazards?

We first came to this question in the course of our graduate studies, while writing dissertations on the regulation of risky technologies. We found an enormous literature on the subject, but little that would help us reach a systematic judgment. Technical work on the subject was nearly unintelligible and did not directly address our questions; studies by risk analysts showed much less respect for uncertainty and human error than political scientists could find plausible; and the claims of critics and supporters of various risky endeavors seemed patently biased.

To our surprise, moreover, we found a large gap in knowledge of how society actually regulates risky technologies. If there are strategies in use, nowhere are they carefully described. If there are sensible prescriptions that might improve these strategies, nowhere are they clearly articulated. If there is reason for confidence in society's ability to avert future catastrophes, nowhere is it laid out simply and systematically. For political scientists, this was an astounding state of affairs, for one of our central beliefs is that a good decision-making process is the best guarantor of good policies. Until we know what process is being used to make decisions about technological risks, there is no way to decide whether a society is making sensible decisions. Hence this book, in which we explain how risky technologies now are being handled. This volume is intended for a very diverse audience:

For general readers without a technical background, it offers a readily intelligible description of risky technologies and how society copes with them.

For students in environmental politics, science-technology-society, policy analysis, and other courses, this volume offers a set of case studies on the regulation of risky technologies.

For decision theorists, we offer a study of decision making in the face of high uncertainty and potentially catastrophic consequences.

For scientists and engineers, we describe the logic of society's approach to risky technologies—a process that so often strikes technically-minded people as devoid of logic and good sense.

For scientists and risk analysts who have been at the forefront of recent technical controversies, the facts here will not be new; but the strategies we discuss may prove interesting—and our criticisms of risk analysis certainly will be controversial.

We owe our primary intellectual debt to Charles E. Lindblom, for whom we worked at Yale's Institution for Social and Policy Studies. Only the largest and most penetrating questions interested him, so we strived to develop such questions. Errors of style annoyed him, so we had to learn to eliminate them. He was almost impossible to impress, so to earn an occasional bit of grudging praise, we had to stretch our capacities beyond what we considered reasonable. During times when we were disappointed in the irrelevance of much academic scholarship to pressing human problems, his work served as a reminder that political science could be useful. Finally, to our surprise, this man's ideas somehow found their way to the core of our perceptions about social life. This book is dedicated to him.

Approximately thirty staff members from the Environmental Protection Agency, National Institutes of Health, National Research Council, relevant interest groups, congressional offices, and other organizations gave generously of their time and knowledge in interviews—most in person, some by telephone. Morone benefitted from an Industrial Research Institute fellowship at the Office of Science and Technology Policy during 1984, and Woodhouse received travel and research support from the Rensselaer Polytechnic Institute (RPI) Department of Science and Technology Studies.

The manuscript has been read and critiqued at various stages by too many people to acknowledge all individually. Special thanks are due, however, to Aaron Wildavsky, who went out of his way to offer encouragement and helpful advice at a time when the project was in difficulty. Richard Alben, Ralph Alpher, Leroy Gould, Henry Hurwitz, Roland Schmitt, Myron Uman, and Richard Young offered especially constructive criticisms on significant portions of the manuscript. Several hundred RPI undergraduate science and engineering majors provided helpful feedback on various drafts of the manuscript in the process of learning about the political side of their future professions.

We profited from the advice of technical writers Barbara Corman and Monica Fabian in making the scientific materials readily accessible to a wide audience. University of California Press editors Ernest Callenbach, Evelyn Mercer Ward, and Marilyn Schwartz impressed us by their swiftness and professionalism during the publication process. Bob Fairchild provided excellent research assistance. For word processing, we thank Marge McLeod of RPI.

Finally, for sustained emotional support, and incredible pa-

tience when writing came at the expense of already scarce time
with his family, Morone expresses deep gratitude to his wife,
Lindsay Evans. This book is also dedicated to her.

Joseph G. Morone
General Electric Corporate
   Research and Development
Schenectady, New York

Edward J. Woodhouse
Department of Science and
   Technology Studies
Rensselaer Polytechnic
Institute, Troy, NY

1

The Potential for Catastrophe

Americans are bombarded almost daily with news of potential and actual catastrophe, ranging from individual automobile accidents and homicides to collective disasters such as famines and earthquakes. War and terrorism are not rare either, with nuclear conflagration now the ultimate fear. Increasingly in the past two decades, however, a different sort of potential catastrophe has gained prominence—environmental threats that could lead to massive human health problems and to irreversible deterioration of the global ecosystem. This volume focuses on these environmental threats and on efforts to avert them.

Particular sources of environmental threats are legion and headlines shift accordingly, year to year, month to month. In 1962 Rachel Carson's *Silent Spring* sounded an alarm about DDT poisoning in fish, wildlife, and humans. In 1971 opponents of the supersonic transport asserted that the jet's exhaust could disrupt the upper atmosphere, with potentially severe consequences for global weather patterns. In 1974 two scientists reported that fluorocarbon aerosol sprays might deplete atmospheric ozone and cause millions of cases of skin cancer. Other scientists meanwhile warned that harmful bacteria could escape into the general population during the conduct of new biological experiments.

Shortly thereafter reports from Love Canal sparked investigations into thousands of abandoned waste dumps containing chemicals that might cause birth defects, cancer, and other serious illnesses. Nuclear power plants became increasingly controversial during the 1970s, and fears about their safety escalated after the Three Mile Island accident in 1979. Public attention subsequently shifted to acid rain and then to the pesticide EDB. In late 1984 several thousand people were killed and nearly two hundred thousand were injured when a pesticide chemical leaked into the air from a Union Carbide chemical plant in Bhopal, India—the worst civilian technological disaster in history.

This long list of incidents has had a substantial effect on the public's perception of government's capacity to cope with risky technologies. For example, while pro- and anti-nuclear factions disagree on almost every substantive issue, both generally agree that the nuclear regulatory process has not been working. One side sees the Nuclear Regulatory Commission as hamstringing a vital industry offering a viable alternative to limited supplies of fossil fuels. The other side perceives the Commission as so biased toward the industry's viewpoint that public health and safety are endangered. Roughly the same perceptions characterize government action on toxic chemicals. Across these and many other areas of risk regulation, a common view is that government has bungled, and bungled badly.

The many actual and potential environmental dangers raise concerns about the way we interact with our ecosystem. Prominent environmentalists and other social thinkers have issued dire injunctions about fundamental changes we must make to avoid ruining the earth. Barry Commoner, for example, wrote in *The Closing Circle* in 1971: "We are in an environmental crisis because the means by which we use the ecosphere to produce wealth are destructive of the ecosphere itself. The present system of production is self-destructive; the present course of human civilization is suicidal."[1] In *The Coming Dark Age,* the Italian intellectual Roberto Vacca argues that "vast concentrations of human beings are involved in systems that are now so complicated that they are becoming uncontrollable."[2] Theodore Roszak's *Where the Wasteland Ends* speaks of

the varieties of annihilation . . . the thermonuclear Armageddon, the death of the seas, the vanishing atmosphere, the massacre of the innocents, the universal famine to come. . . .
Such horrors should be the stuff of nightmare or the merely metaphorical rancors of old prophecy. They aren't. They are the news of the day, by now even growing stale (for some) with reiteration.[3]

And the respected historian of technology Lewis Mumford claimed in 1970 that

the professional bodies that should have been monitoring our technology . . . have been criminally negligent in anticipating or even reporting what has actually been taking place. . . . [Technological society is] a purely mechanical system whose processes can neither be redirected nor halted, that has no internal mechanism for warning of defects or correcting them.[4]

Such opinions are extreme, but many other thoughtful observers of the human condition have expressed serious forebodings about environmental catastrophe. There is also another reason for concern, and that is that preventing an ecocatastrophe cannot always be accomplished by trial and error. Social scientists who study decision making generally agree that trial and error is a necessary component in human decision making about complex problems. However sophisticated the analysis and planning is that goes into a decision, uncertainties at the outset ordinarily are so great that errors are inevitable. It is by paying attention to these errors once they become apparent that individuals, organizations, and governments learn how to improve their choices.[5] Unfortunately, the environmental problems that can lead to ecocatastrophe have several characteristics that make them unusually difficult to ameliorate with a trial-and-error approach.[6]

The "trials" in some environmental policies often affect very large areas—even the entire globe—placing billions of people potentially at risk. Thus, errors in environmental policy can have potentially catastrophic consequences (for instance, a cancer epidemic) and waiting for errors to emerge before correcting policy therefore appears to be an unpromising regulatory strategy.

Moreover, when errors are made, they may result in consequences that are partially or wholly irreversible; such is the case
with contaminated drinking water aquifers that take centuries
to regenerate, the extinction of a species crucial to a significant
food chain, and improper disposal of nuclear and toxic wastes
that can affect humans and animals for very long periods.

In addition, because correcting an error requires that first
an error and its consequences be recognized, the long lag time
prior to feedback (that is, emergence of information about
errors) can prevent for many years the realization that a problem even exists. It took some twenty-five years for persuasive
evidence about the harmful effects of DDT to accumulate;
evidence on lead and asbestos required even longer. It is not
only that delayed feedback results in the accumulation of undesired consequences over the period required for the error to
become apparent, but that, as a group of global modelers
reports: "Owing to the momentum inherent in the world's
physical and social processes, policy changes made soon are
likely to have more impact with less effort than the same set of
changes made later. By the time a problem is obvious to
everyone, it is often too late to solve it."[7]

Finally, there are so many potential sources of important
problems that the sheer number may interfere with effective
monitoring of emerging errors. For example, there are more
than sixty thousand chemicals now commercially used in the
United States. The result, according to a respected group of
professional risk assessors, is that "if hazards are dealt with
one at a time, many must be neglected. The instinctive response to this problem is to deal with problems in order of
importance. Unfortunately, the information needed to establish priorities is not available; the collection of such data might
itself swamp the system."[8]

The predicament is that society is wrestling with risky technologies whose inherent nature makes them difficult to regulate by the traditional process of trial, error, and correction of
error. Since error correction is the key to good decision making on complex issues, social scientists offer at least partial
support on this particular point for the concerns of critics of
environmental policy.

Recent Health and Safety Experience

Given the warnings of environmentalists and the theoretical concerns of social scientists, we would expect to see severe health and safety problems resulting from the risky technologies deployed increasingly during the twentieth century. In fact, health and safety trends to date do not match this expectation.[9] Interpretations vary, of course, and there certainly is ample room for improvement in health and safety measures. But given the challenge posed by modern technologies, the record to date is surprisingly good: despite dire warnings, no catastrophes have occurred in the United States.

Civilian nuclear power provides a good example. Clearly it has not become an energy source "too cheap to meter," as one early advocate is said to have forecast. Moreover, the nuclear power issue is a source of tension and conflict in American society. Yet nuclear reactors have been operating for more than two decades without significant adverse effects on public health. This record is especially impressive since it was achieved in the context of a policy-making process centered in the Atomic Energy Commission that many now consider to have been badly flawed because of inadequate outside scrutiny.[10]

By all accounts, Three Mile Island was the worst reactor mishap in the history of the American nuclear industry, and it was a financial disaster for the utility that owned the plant. But from a safety perspective, the accident was about the equivalent of a car accident. Some radiation was released, but the average dose to Pennsylvania residents within fifty miles of Three Mile Island (TMI) was less than 1 percent of the average background radiation to which they are exposed each year.[11] The accident revealed a plethora of faults—poor management, maintenance errors, operator errors, and design errors (see chapter 3)—but even these did not lead to severe consequences for public health.

Widespread use of toxic chemicals also causes public alarm. The United States took the lead in introducing into the ecosystem hundreds of billions of pounds of inorganic and synthetic organic chemicals. At the outset we knew virtually nothing about the effects of these chemicals on human health, wildlife,

ocean life, microbial processes, and other aspects of the ecosystem. Ecocatastrophe might well have resulted from such
unexamined and widespread use of toxic substances. To date,
however, it has not. Because pesticides are designed to be
toxic and are deliberately sprayed into the ecosystem, they
provide an especially good example of a potential ecocatastrophe. By most standards, the average consumer in the
United States has less to worry about from the effects of pesticides during the 1980s than in the 1960s or perhaps even in the
1940s.[12] The same appears to be true in occupational and consumer exposures to toxic substances, although the data on this
are currently inadequate.

But what about rising cancer rates? Have we already made
millions of people ill by our toxic substances policies? There is
no question that cancer is more frequent now than it was a
century ago. But the change in cancer rates since synthetic
chemicals came into common use is of a different nature than
many realize. Lung cancer has increased rapidly, primarily
from cigarette smoking. Digestive and cervical cancer have
dropped significantly, and breast cancer death rates are stable.
These types of cancer together account for about 75 percent of
all cancer deaths. Rates of some other forms of cancer have
declined slightly, and some have increased moderately; only a
few types of cancer, such as mesothelioma (from asbestos) and
melanoma (skin cancer), have increased dramatically. So there
is no overall cancer epidemic, and some of the observed increase is due to increased longevity. In some occupations and
in certain geographical areas, of course, exposures to asbestos
or other dangerous substances have been much greater than
the nationwide average, and higher local incidences of cancer
have been the result.[13]

To the extent that cancer is caused by environmental exposures, chemicals were the prime suspects in the popular media during the early and mid-1970s. Most cancer researchers,
however, put industrial and consumer chemicals relatively far
down on the list of carcinogens. Tobacco comes first, closely
followed by the high-fat modern diet; alcohol and radiation
(primarily sunlight and natural background radiation) rank
next. Then in fifth place comes occupational and consumer

use of chemicals, along with air and water pollution; this amounts to 4 to 10 percent of cancer deaths according to most careful estimates.[14] Much of this fraction is caused by such occupational hazards as asbestos, mining, welding, woodworking, and coke oven emissions. Some of these cancers involve chemicals, but they are not the synthetic organic chemicals that we ordinarily associate with the toxic chemicals problem. So the overall effects of synthetic chemicals to date have not been catastrophic.[15]

Recombinant DNA (rDNA) research offers another example. During the mid-1970s, the prospect of splicing genetic material from one organism into another triggered fears of new and virulent epidemic diseases. Yet rDNA research has a perfect safety record to date; there have been thousands of experiments without any known health problems. However, the field is still in its early stages and is now moving from the laboratory into the environment where there are new risks. But experience to date is so reassuring that the burden of proof is now on those who believe this research involves unreasonable risks. Such critics are few, though some observers fear the release into the environment of newly created organisms (such as microbes that eat oil spills), and others are concerned about the increase in scale of recombinant procedures from small laboratory-scale experiments to industrial-size vats. Nevertheless, to date, the safety record is a good one.

It is possible to cite other examples, but by now the point should be clear: despite justifiable warnings and widespread public fears about the risks of complex new technologies, our society so far has escaped most of the predicted damage to human health.

A System for Averting Catastrophe?

How has this relatively good health and safety record been achieved? It is not the outcome many people expected. One possibility is that we simply have been lucky. Or perhaps the unhappy consequences from these technologies have not yet fully emerged (cancers from use of chemicals in the past twenty years still could show up, for example). A third possibility is that idiosyncratic reactions to particular dangers have served to avoid the worst outcomes, but there has been no carryover of learning from one type of risk to another. If this is true, there is little assurance that the next danger will be averted. Finally, it is conceivable that the good record somehow is a systematic product of human actions—the result of a deliberate process by which risks are monitored, evaluated, and reduced.

The purpose of this volume is to explore this last possibility. In the chapters that follow, we examine the regulation of five types of technological risks: toxic chemicals, nuclear power, recombinant DNA research, threats to the ozone layer, and the greenhouse effect. In each chapter we will attempt to discern the strategies pursued in diagnosing and attempting to avert these threats.

At the outset of this research, we approached this subject with the commonly held assumption that the United States had botched the job of regulating risky technologies. Yet when we actually delved into how regulators have coped with the various risks, we discovered a surprisingly intelligent process. That is not to say the outcomes are fully satisfactory; but the strategies are far more sensible than we expected. The strategies we found usually were not fully developed. Nor were they always implemented effectively. And, in most of our cases, some useful strategies were ignored or underemphasized. But taken together, the strategies we found in use suggest the elements of a complete system for averting catastrophe. This system has five main elements.

First, an obvious early step is to protect against potential catastrophes. Part of this effort aims at preventing problems from occurring. But since the threats usually are too complex to fully envision and avoid, it is necessary to devise protections that limit the damage. We found considerable effort devoted to this goal in four of our five cases, although very different tactics are employed in each.

Because of the great uncertainty about the likelihood and magnitude of potential catastrophes, a second and related strategy is to proceed cautiously in protecting against potential catastrophes. Decision makers can assume the worst rather than expect the likely. On this count, our cases display a mixed pattern. While there are important examples of such caution, we believe it would have been better to be more conservative about some of these risks.

A third strategy is to actively attempt to reduce uncertainty about the likelihood and magnitude of potential harm by testing whenever possible, rather than simply waiting to learn from experience via trial and error. Such testing is employed extensively in our cases and proves useful in preventing or limiting some potentially severe and irreversible errors.

Because the number of risks is too large to devote equal attention to all, a fourth step is to set priorities. Explicit procedures to achieve this end have been developed for some aspects of toxic chemicals, but less formal processes for priority setting are used for other types of risk. For at least one risky technology we studied, we found a clear opportunity for better priority setting than has been employed to date.

A fifth element is learning from experience, and we were surprised to find how much of this has occurred. In part because the ecosystem (so far) has been more forgiving than reasonably might be expected, learning from previous errors has been an important component of the system for averting catastrophe.

As we examine the regulatory histories of the five cases of technological risk, we consider each of these five strategies: protection against severe risks, erring on the side of caution, advance testing, priority setting, and learning from error. In each case our objective is to examine how potential catastrophes have been averted and to learn what strategies have been developed that can be applied to future problems.

Preview of the Analysis

Our inquiry begins in chapter 2 and concerns regulations governing the use of toxic chemicals. The questions considered are (1) How were toxic chemicals regulated prior to the emergence of public environmental consciousness?

(2) What efforts have been made since 1970 to improve on early regulatory strategies? (3) Do these new programs appear to be succeeding? This chapter shows the surprising effectiveness of trial-and-error as well as two other decision-making techniques that improve on this strategy.

Chapter 3 is about nuclear power. The potential for catastrophe here is strikingly different from that posed by toxic substances: the effects of a nuclear power plant accident would be highly concentrated. Therefore, the risk-reduction strategies that have evolved are at least superficially quite different from those for toxic substances. The chapter reviews safety procedures that evolved during the 1950s and 1960s; the Three Mile Island accident is then analyzed as a test case of those procedures.

The fourth chapter concerns an aspect of research in genetic engineering—recombinant DNA—in which DNA is taken from one organism and spliced into another. During the mid-1970s this procedure was as controversial as nuclear power; it was feared that some genetically altered bacteria would escape from laboratories and negatively impact human health or the environment. These and other concerns all but disappeared by the end of the decade, at least partly because of the development of rules for and safeguards against this possible hazard. This is our most definitive case, and in this chapter we come close to realizing the complete catastrophe-aversion system in operation.

Chapter 5 considers a threat to the global atmosphere—chemical assaults on the ozone layer that filters out a portion of ultraviolet light before it reaches the earth's surface. In 1970 several scientists suggested that flights by supersonic transports (SSTs) through the stratosphere might reduce atmospheric ozone. Subsequent investigations revealed a number of other ways that human activities might deplete ozone and thereby lead to substantial increases in rates of skin cancer and to changes in global climate. The focus of this chapter is on the scientific monitoring system that diagnosed these dangers and on the strategies that evolved to cope with them.

The subject of chapter six is a threat that poses no threat of actual harm for at least half a century—the greenhouse effect, a gradual warming of the earth's climate and the shift in weather patterns caused by increased carbon dioxide and other trace gases in the atmosphere, due in part to combustion of fossil fuels. This case provides another look at the implicit strategy of using scientists to monitor technological risks and considers the real problem of how to balance risks against benefits. This chapter also raises disturbing questions about government's ability to avert global risks when these involve central aspects of our way of life.

In chapter 7 we formulate and discuss the complete catastrophe-aversion system, first describing the major elements of the system, their variations, and how each was applied in the toxic chemicals, nuclear power, recombinant DNA, ozone, and greenhouse effect cases. We then consider how our findings can be used to improve decision making about both risky technologies and other matters of policy.

In the concluding chapter we discuss prospects for improved application of the catastrophe-aversion system. One major complaint about contemporary risk management concerns the problem "How safe is safe enough?" Implementation of safety precautions is a matter of degree, and each additional precaution typically involves increased cost. One prominent school of thought holds that sensible decisions about "How safe?" can best be made by improving risk analysis. We explain why this is a dubious hope, and we propose a more strategic approach to improving the catastrophe-aversion system.

Caveats

Before turning to the subject of toxic chemicals in chapter 2, some clarification about the scope of our analysis is in order. Even though we consider a fairly wide array of risks, we make no claim to comprehensiveness. This volume analyzes selected aspects of the regulatory histories of selected technologies. There are too many potential technological catastrophes to include them all, and each of our cases is complex enough to justify its own separate work. But an extended analysis of the five technological risks reviewed here should prove useful in spite of the necessary selectivity.

This volume is also selective in that it focuses on the United States. There is much to be learned about other nations' responses to technologies with a potential for catastrophe, both for their own sake and to illuminate the strengths and weaknesses of U.S. responses. But undertaking such comparisons would have required a much different study than we have undertaken.

We do not attempt to cover the politics—interest group maneuvering, partisan lineups in Congress, the role of the media, struggles within regulatory agencies, details of litigation, or changes in public opinion—of each controversy. However fascinating, these are short-term phenomena, and our aim is to uncover deeper patterns, namely, regulatory strategies that endure.

The focus of this volume is restricted to civilian technologies that could result in unintentional harm. We do not include casualties and other damages that humans inflict on one another through military technologies. The potential for military-induced catastrophes almost surely is greater than for civilian technologies, and there is much to be learned about how to prevent such tragedies; this is not our topic here.

Also, our subject is severe threats. We take it for granted that some people will be harmed by almost every human activity (coins, for example, are dangerous household items because toddlers can swallow them). While we use no precise measure to distinguish severe threats from milder ones, we are concerned with those threats that potentially involve thousands of deaths annually rather than tens or hundreds. That is not to say that lesser risks are unimportant or acceptable, but they are not in the scope of this volume.

Our analysis is restricted to physical threats to the environment and to human health and safety. There are other threats raised by contemporary civilian technologies, some of which may be even more important to human well-being than physical health and safety. Some unions, for example, are concerned that widespread introduction of industrial robots could lead to significant unemployment, at least for the short term, among certain classes of workers. Likewise, some modern biomedical procedures are perceived by many people to violate deeply held values. Such issues are important and deserve more attention, but they are not part of this inquiry.

Finally, this volume aims to be as unpoliticized as possible. While we have (sometimes opposing) political opinions on the subjects discussed, we have striven to keep these out of our analysis. We desire this book to be equally useful to pro- and anti-nuclear readers, to pro-growth advocates as well as to ardent environmentalists, to conservatives and to liberals. We are not attempting to change anyone's mind about any particular political controversy. Rather our aim is to clarify the strategies that have been evolving for coping with potential environmental threats that almost everyone agrees must be addressed in some manner. To the extent that regulators and other political participants have a clear perspective of the strategies that have been used to avert catastrophes, judicious application of these strategies in future controversies becomes more likely.

This book, then, examines how our society has learned to deal with the potential for catastrophe created by modern technology. If we are to have at least modest confidence in humanity's future, we must have a reasonable hope that severe physical threats from civilian technologies can be managed without unacceptable harm to human health or the ecosystem. We must know how decisions affecting health and safety get made. Are we learning how to avert catastrophes in general? Are policy makers discovering how to learn about environmental problems? And are they learning how to use such improved abilities to actually avert potential future problems?

2

Toxic Chemicals

Love Canal led to widespread concern over improper disposal of toxic substances, and the 1984 disaster at Bhopal, India, spotlighted the risks of chemical manufacturing plants. But manufacture and disposal may actually be easier to regulate than the daily use of chemicals by millions of people throughout the economy. This chapter examines how the U.S. government, scientists, environmentalists, and industries have worked (and failed to work) to circumvent disaster from careless use of toxic chemicals.

Regulation of chemicals offers an excellent test of society's ability to avert potential catastrophes. Beginning with the industrial revolution and increasing sharply in the twentieth century, technological societies began to introduce into the ecosystem chemicals with unknown consequences for natural systems and human health. The quantities of chemicals introduced are staggering: U. S. production of synthetic organic chemicals has escalated from virtually zero in 1918 to more than 228 billion pounds annually. Reliance on inorganic chemicals such as asbestos also has increased significantly. In total, there are more than sixty thousand chemicals now in use.

Until recently, the primary approach to regulation has been a trial-and-error process. Few restrictions were placed on the production and use of chemicals. Judgments about the purposes to which a chemical should be put, the manner and frequency of its application, and its potency were left largely unregulated until actual experience provided evidence of serious risk. But a more deliberate approach to protecting against potential hazards now has emerged. The two most important strategies are to test new chemicals before they come on the market and to set priorities for regulating toxic substances already in use.

Learning by Trial and Error: Pesticides

The essence of learning from error is to try something, observe the outcome, and try something new to correct any undesirable results. The regulatory history of pesticides is one of learning from error; the central theme in this history is the emergence of feedback about errors and society's response to this feedback. Two of the main types of feedback resulted from environmental problems and human health concerns. (The term "feedback" in this volume refers to the process whereby errors in a policy or course of action become apparent.)

Effects on the environment

Beekeepers began to notice damage to their bee populations soon after the introduction of inorganic pesticides in the 1870s. Because their livelihood depended on pollination of their crops, orchardists were keenly interested in the beekeepers' problems. Although initially skeptical, people paid attention to the beekeepers' claims, and early entomologists carried out simple tests confirming the allegations. In one such test, a tree and its bees were enclosed in netting and sprayed as usual; a high percentage of the bees died. By the 1890s agricultural extension experts were advising farmers to delay application of pesticides until after trees had finished blossoming—and orchardists quickly followed the advice.[1]

Another example of negative feedback first appeared in the 1880s when London Purple supplanted Paris Green as the favorite insecticide of American agriculturalists (the active ingredient in both was arsenic). A waste byproduct of the British aniline dye industry, London Purple was so highly toxic that it actually harmed the plants to which it was applied. When experience with lead arsenate (developed to fight gypsy moths in 1892) demonstrated that plant burn was not inevitable, a combination of market forces and governmental action gradually steered pesticide developers toward chemical preparations less destructive to plants.[2]

Recurrent complaints about illnesses and deaths of livestock were a third source of learning. Incidents that were investigated appear to have been accidents caused by careless use or mislabeling, rather than from correct application. Even when negative feedback is misinterpreted in such cases, it can still prove useful. While these incidents did not reveal the errors originally supposed (that normal use of pesticides was a danger to livestock), the controversies raised consciousness about the possibility of real dangers, and this stimulated development of scientific testing methods.

The possibility of damage to soil fertility was perceived almost immediately after the introduction of inorganic insecticides in the 1860s. A few early tests accurately indicated cause for concern, but other tests showing more reassuring results got wider publicity and acceptance. Some farmers and agricultural experts issued recurrent warnings, such as this one from an 1891 issue of *Garden and Forest:* "Hundreds of tons of a most virulent poison in the hands of hundreds of thousands of people, to be freely used in fields, orchards and gardens all over the continent, will incur what in the aggregate must be a danger worthy of serious thought."[3] There was bitter opposition to use of new chemicals in many rural areas. Nevertheless, inorganic pesticides won steadily increasing acceptance as a standard part of agricultural practice, apparently because the immediate feedback (increased usable crop yields) was positive.

By the 1920s, however, soils in some orchards had accumulated concentrations of arsenic as high as 600 parts per million (ppm), more than forty times the amount that occurs in nature. Newly planted trees were difficult to keep alive, and crop yields declined. For example, in the soil of some rice-growing areas of the Mississippi Valley, high levels of arsenic remain from past pesticide applications, causing rice plants to abort and resulting in poor crop yields. The one positive result is that such damage helped stimulate research on other pesticides to replace lead-arsenic compounds.[4]

The damage to wildlife caused by insecticides drew public attention when, in 1962 in *Silent Spring,* Rachel Carson pointed out the high economic and aesthetic costs of DDT and revealed that other new persistent insecticides were killing birds, fish, and other wildlife.[5] She quoted startling statistics showing pesticide concentrations over 2,000 parts per million in California waterfowl; Michigan robins killed by DDT had 200 ppm in their oviducts, and their eggs were contaminated.[6] Even though there was no standard for evaluating such findings, most readers were shocked. Moreover, Carson documented hundreds of separate incidents of fish, shrimp, oysters, and other valuable aquatic organisms killed by dieldrin, endrin, DDT, and other chlorinated hydrocarbon pesticides; the largest kills each totalled over one million fish.[7]

The emergence of pesticide-resistant insects offered further evidence of error. At least eight instances of pests becoming resistant to insecticides were recorded prior to 1940. Houseflies became resistant to DDT in Sweden by 1946, just two years after the chemical's introduction there. By the mid-1970s over three hundred species of pest arthropods had developed resistances to one or more pesticides; some were resistant to as many as a dozen different chemicals.[8]

Because this was a major problem for the agricultural sector, corporate, government, and university scientists began intensive research on how insects develop immunity. Resulting knowledge about insects and the biochemistry of pesticides led to improved agricultural policy. For example, scientists developed the concept of selection pressure, which holds that the more frequent the spraying and the more persistent the pesticide used, the more rapid the development of resistance in the pest population. This concept and the resistance problem led to a search for less persistent pesticides and to efforts to develop biological control methods intended to reduce agricultural losses by affecting pest fertility, bypassing insects' chemical defenses.

Human exposures and responses

Because they sometimes were visible and drew consumers' attention, pesticide residues on fruits and vegetables were a prime source of feedback and learning about the timing and advisable limits of chemical spraying. Early experimenters generally agreed that the risk of immediate poisoning from residues was quite small, but it was not until 1887 that the possibility of chronic illness from cumulative exposures was suggested.

Several well-publicized incidents in Britain between 1891 and 1900, sensationalized by the media, directed the attention of medical and governmental authorities to the problem of chemical residues. This led to the establishment of British and world tolerances (levels generally accepted as safe) for arsenic residues.

In the United States, seizures of contaminated produce by local governments sparked the beginning of serious regulation. In 1919 the Boston City Health Department began a series of seizures of western apples and pears, some contaminated with more than twenty times the residue levels considered acceptable in world commerce. The Bureau of Chemistry in the U. S. Department of Agriculture (USDA) made a decade-long attempt to educate American growers about the problem but met with little success. In 1925 southern New Jersey and Philadelphia experienced an epidemic illness that newspapers attributed to spray residues on fruits. These claims turned out to be incorrect, but federal inspectors did find apples with very high residue levels. When New Jersey growers refused to clean the affected apples, the first actual seizure and destruction of produce under the Food and Drugs Act of 1906 took place.

In late 1925 and early 1926 British newspapers published nearly a thousand cartoons, articles, and editorials lambasting arsenic-contaminated American fruit. The incident started when a family became ill from arsenic poisoning caused by imported U.S. apples; subsequent inspections revealed contaminated American fruit throughout Britain. The British government threatened a complete embargo on U.S. produce, causing the U.S.-based International Apple Shippers Association to take measures limiting arsenic levels on export fruit. Produce for domestic consumption in the United States also gradually improved owing to improved washing techniques and longer delays between spraying and harvest. Nonetheless, residue levels remained higher in the United States than those allowed in Britain because of the strong farm lobby in Congress.[9]

Several lessons were learned from this case. The concept of tolerance (a level of poison that most people could consume daily without becoming ill) was developed and gradually incorporated into legal standards. Dissatisfaction with initial enforcement of these standards led to stricter enforcement, which led to improved techniques for washing fruit and other methods for keeping residue levels close to legal standards. Finally, various farmers' organizations began to demand the development of insecticides that would be as effective as arsenic but less toxic.

Knowledge and regulation of pesticides also increased as a result of data on human exposures. While the average person had a DDT level of 5 to 7 parts per million (ppm) in the late 1950s, farm workers were found to store an average of 17.1 ppm, and the highest recorded level, 648 ppm, was found in an insecticide plant worker. These figures approximately doubled in the 1960s.[10] Although laboratory evidence showed that minute concentrations of pesticides could inhibit human enzyme and oxidation processes, there was no solid evidence that these changes would lead to serious human illness. Some methodologically weak studies even showed that high doses were safe.[11] Nevertheless, statistics on occupational exposure levels, like those on insecticides' effects on wildlife, alarmed many people.

In 1974 the Environmental Protection Agency (EPA) approved the pesticide leptophos for use on lettuce and tomatoes, despite evidence suggesting that leptophos caused nervous disorders. When workers in a Bayport, Texas, plant that manufactured the chemical experienced severe nervous disorders, EPA quickly rescinded its approval, after the media publicized the incident, and the plant ceased production of the pesticide.

In 1975 workers at a Hopewell, Virginia, chemical manufacturing plant owned by Allied Chemical were found to suffer from brain and liver disorders and from other serious ailments caused by the chemical kepone. Investigation revealed that the plant had been illegally discharging dangerous effluents into the James River for the previous three years. As a result, the river was closed to commercial fishing for several years, and Allied Chemical was fined $5 million and required to donate an additional $8 million for environmental research.

These incidents were significant in themselves, and contributed to tightening occupational health safeguards in the pesticide industry. More generally, the kepone and leptophos problems directed media, interest group, and congressional attention to the toxic substances problem.

Results of trial and error

The use of trial and error has been more effective in the regulation of pesticides than we initially believed possible. There have been many errors, much feedback about them, and numerous efforts to learn from these errors.[12] The lag time between trial and feedback has been long, but this has only slowed rather than prevented the learning process.

The result is that most of us appear to be safer today from pesticides than we were a generation or two ago. The currently used carbamate and organophosphate pesticides are much less persistent, and therefore much less dangerous to consumers' health and the ecosystem, than were the chlorinated hydrocarbon and arsenic-lead-fluorine pesticides.[13] Levels of DDT and other persistent pesticide residues in food came uncomfortably close to the accepted tolerance limit in 1970. In contrast, recent readings on levels of the organophosphate chemical malathion show expected daily intake in the United States to be less than 1 percent of the tolerance limit. Residue levels for carbaryl (the major carbamate pesticide) are even lower.[14] Not everyone accepts such official standards of safety, but most of the trends are reassuring.

Even though the trial-and-error method has worked to a considerable extent for pesticides, the strategy is clearly of limited utility—particularly when considering the larger universe of chemicals. Only about six hundred different chemicals are used in contemporary pesticides, and less than a third of these predominate. Therefore, it is much easier to monitor feedback about them than to keep track of all sixty thousand chemicals in use today. Moreover, we cannot say that trial and error has worked well enough, even for pesticides. The harm has been substantial, and perhaps partially irreversible.[15] Revelations of damage from various types of chemicals, the gradual emergence of the field of toxicology, and popular books such as *100,000,000 Guinea Pigs* in the 1930s and *Silent Spring* in the 1960s, prompted doubts about the trial-and-error process. Slowly, more deliberate strategies began to emerge to supplement trial and error.

Early Steps to Supplement Trial and Error

The first federal laws dealing with toxic chemicals were the 1906 Food and Drugs Act and the 1910 Federal Insecticide Act.[16] Both laws were based purely on trial and error: they gave federal agencies authority to seize an adulterated substance only *after* it had been marketed in interstate commerce. The government then had to prove in court that the product exceeded legal toxic limits.

The 1938 Food, Drug, and Cosmetic Act was the first law to mandate a major change in strategy—testing of substances *before* they were sold. The intention was to obtain information about ineffective or dangerous chemicals before dangerous effects could occur. (This applied only to pharmaceuticals.)

The 1947 Federal Insecticide, Fungicide, and Rodenticide Act (FIFRA) extended the advance testing requirement to pesticides. It required registration with the Food and Drug Administration (FDA), prior to marketing, of any pesticide products sold in interstate commerce. To obtain such registration, manufacturers had to submit the results of toxicity tests on their pesticides. The effect of this legislation was to shift to manufacturers part of the burden of proving the safety of pesticide products sold in interstate commerce. Previously, FDA had been forced into onerous litigation and required to assume the burden of proving in court that a pesticide was sufficiently dangerous to justify removing it from the market. The new requirements on manufacturers thus helped reduce the probability of dangerous chemicals remaining on the market. FIFRA also represented a first step toward another new strategy—adding an element of caution to the way in which chemicals are introduced and used in society.

The Delaney Amendment of 1958 and the Color Additives Amendments of 1960 represented the clearest examples of this conservative strategy. More than any previous legislation, the Color Additives Amendments put the burden of proving safety squarely on the manufacturer.[17] The Delaney Amendment specified that no chemical additive shown to cause cancer in laboratory animals could be added to food. It instructed FDA to accept animal tests that may not always be valid for humans and to treat even mildly carcinogenic substances the same as potent ones. If there are to be errors in how society introduces and uses chemicals, the 1958 law implied, it is better to err on the side of safety. However, as we will discuss in chapter 8, this attempt to impose caution proved too conservative to be workable.

The 1954 Pesticide Chemicals Amendment introduced a third strategy. It empowered the Department of Agriculture and FDA for the first time to ban the use of excessively dangerous pesticides. Complaints abounded, however, that the existing system's procedures stifled effective action by the regulatory agencies. So FIFRA was amended repeatedly, each time easing procedures for banning or limiting pesticides the regulatory agencies considered too dangerous. For example, a controversy over the herbicide 2, 4, 5–T led the director of the White House Office of Science and Technology to complain in 1970 that "there is not sufficient flexibility [in the laws] . . . to allow the government to take action" expeditiously when new information reveals unforeseen health hazards.[18] The 1972 Federal Environmental Pesticide Control Act partially eased this difficulty, reducing the required burden of proof that a pesticide posed an unreasonable risk. The act allowed EPA to block registration of a pesticide as long as evidence does not clearly demonstrate that benefits outweigh risks.[19]

The 1972 act also divided pesticides into categories, corresponding roughly to prescription versus nonprescription drugs. In an effort to guard against errors due to incompetent application, use of the more dangerous pesticides henceforth could be restricted to individuals and firms certified by EPA. The act also provided for indemnity payments to manufacturers of pesticides that EPA orders off the market. This provision dilutes opposition to banning dangerous chemicals and thus makes regulatory action easier and potentially quicker.

Strategies for New Toxic Substances

The early trial-and-error process in the use of toxic chemicals, then, was followed by a trial-and-error process in regulation. The laws became increasingly comprehensive, and the regulatory strategies became increasingly sophisticated from 1938 to 1972. But the most significant improvements on trial and error were not developed until the Toxic Substances Control Act (TSCA) of 1976.

The process eventually leading to TSCA began with a 1971 report on toxic substances by the Council on Environmental Quality. Approximately two million chemical compounds were known at that time, and some two hundred fifty thousand new ones were being discovered each year. The great majority of such compounds remained laboratory curiosities that never entered commerce, but approximately one thousand new compounds were believed to be entering the market annually during the late 1960s and early 1970s.[20] An estimated 10 to 20 percent of these new compounds posed environmental threats, as an EPA official later testified to Congress.[21] If this figure was correct, it implied that up to two hundred new environmental hazards might be created each year.

Legislators, environmentalists, and even the chemical industry recognized significant shortcomings in existing laws about toxic substances. Congressional committee reports and floor debates made extensive references to fluorocarbons (chemicals used in spray cans and refrigeration equipment); these chemicals had recently been found to pose a threat to the ozone layer. Also prominent in these discussions were recent incidents involving mercury, lead, vinyl chloride, kepone, and PCBs; the last (widely used as lubricants in electrical equipment) were the only chemicals specifically singled out for special treatment in TSCA. Decision makers also were alarmed by emerging information about environmental sources of cancer (some of it exaggerated); for example, a Senate committee was impressed by "estimates that 60 to 90 percent of the cancers occurring in this country are a result of environmental contaminants. . . . The industrial centers, where industrial chemicals are obviously found in largest concentration, had the highest incidence of cancer."[22]

TSCA's strategies

A central provision of TSCA requires manufacturers to submit premanufacture notices to EPA for each new chemical at least ninety days before commercial production. EPA has the authority to require manufacturers to undertake whatever toxicity testing the agency considers necessary, and EPA is required to ban the manufacture of those new chemicals that present an "unreasonable risk."[23]

A primary motivation behind TSCA, evident throughout the hearings and floor debates, was the desire to prevent excessively dangerous chemicals from being introduced into use—rather than waiting for their negative effects to be observed before removing them from use. As the Senate Commerce Committee put it: "Past experience with certain chemical substances [illustrates] the need for properly assessing the risks of new chemical substances and regulating them *prior* to their introduction."[24] TSCA, the committee said, would "serve as an early warning system." Senator John Tunney (Democrat, California) reiterated the belief that the premarket screening provisions "will assure that we no longer have to *wait for a body count or serious health damage* to generate controls over hazardous chemicals."[25]

The Senate Commerce Committee also acknowledged the social and political consequences of the time lag between introducing a chemical and recognizing its negative effects—the longer the delay in realizing dangers, the more reliant industry becomes on a particular chemical. As the committee report noted, it is prior to first manufacture that

> human suffering, jobs lost, wasted capital expenditures, and other costs are lowest. Frequently, it is far more painful to take regulatory action after all of these costs have been incurred. For example, . . . 1 percent of our gross national product is associated with the vinyl chloride industry. Obviously, it is far more difficult to take regulatory action against this [carcinogenic] chemical now, than it would have been had the dangers been known earlier when alternatives could have been developed and polyvinyl chloride plastics not become such an intrinsic part of our way of life in this country.[26]

As a result of TSCA, manufacturers are now legally required to demonstrate the safety of new chemicals, just as they are for pharmaceuticals, food additives, and pesticides. Any negative evidence, even the sketchiest, may be legally sufficient to keep a new chemical off the market.[27] In practice some risks are considered acceptable if the projected benefits are significant, but uncertainties, if the decision is close, tend to weigh against the side that bears the burden of proof.[28] So TSCA makes strict regulation easier.

Mechanics of premanufacture notification

The premanufacture notification (PMN) system ensures that EPA will have considerable information about a chemical's molecular structure, anticipated production volume in the first few years, by-products, exposure estimates, results of toxicology testing, manufacturing methods, and disposal techniques. EPA can require that industry conduct virtually any tests considered necessary to evaluate a new chemical's safety. Moreover, TSCA grants EPA more authority than ever before to act on the basis of such information.

EPA's review process begins with a structure-activity team of scientists who assign a toxicity rating to each chemical; another group of scientists rates the degree to which individuals and the environment are likely to be exposed to the chemical. If exposure is not rated high and health effects and ecological concerns are all rated low, the chemical passes premanufacture screening. Otherwise the chemical moves to third, fourth, and fifth levels of consideration, with each stage involving higher levels of decision makers and subjecting the chemical to increasing scrutiny.

Initially, the total number of PMN notices submitted was far below the expected amount. This seemed to indicate that industry was launching fewer new chemicals because of the new regulatory requirements. But the number of PMN submissions increased steadily in the early 1980s and leveled off in the range of 1,200 to 1,300 per year.[29]

Year	Submissions
1979	38
1980	366
1981	685
1982	1,059
1983	1,281
1984	1,248

Surprisingly, only about three chemicals out of every ten processed through the PMN system have entered commercial production.[30] According to EPA staff, the chemical companies "invest" in the PMN statement as a stage in research and development, that is, well before a decision has been made to market a chemical. "As soon as prospects for marketing loom on the horizon, they get the PMN in so that marketing will not be held up if the company does decide to go ahead with it."[31] (Some of the submitted PMNs may yet come to market and thus increase the current rate.)

How carefully PMNs are reviewed depends partly on the amount of staff time available for the task. By 1985 there were an equivalent of 125 professional staff and 14 support staff assigned to full-time work on the PMN system. This represented an increase of approximately 21 percent over professional staffing levels of fiscal 1981 and a decrease of about 14 percent in support staff. Meanwhile, expenditures on the PMN

program declined approximately 15 percent in real dollars between 1981 and 1983.[32] While budget allocations and staffing
levels changed moderately, PMN submissions increased substantially. At the 1984 submission rate of 1,250 PMN notices
per year, just over one work month per staff member can be
devoted to each new PMN chemical.

While the PMN program has fared better than other programs at EPA in budget battles (and no doubt efficiency has
improved since the program went into full operation in 1981),
it is questionable whether the current budget is adequate for
the existing workload. The fact that only three chemicals out
of every ten processed by EPA enter commercial production
exacerbates the problem. In effect, scarce EPA time and tal-
ent are being "wasted" on chemicals that companies never
bring to market.

Like most laws, TSCA is changing during implementation.
The legislation explicitly provided authority for EPA to waive
PMN requirements for certain classes of chemicals that are
deemed to pose acceptably low risk and, as a result, numerous
requests for exemption have been submitted. The one that
would cover the most chemicals came from the Chemical
Manufacturers Association in May 1981. It sought exemptions
for high molecular weight polymers, low-volume chemicals of
all kinds, and chemicals that are used only as production intermediates and that remain entirely on the premises of a chemical factory. The Dyes Environmental Toxicology Organization
made a similar request, and also asked that EPA shorten the
review period for various dyes and dye intermediates.[33]

EPA has granted the bulk of the requested exemptions.
Even though manufacturers of an exempted chemical still must
notify EPA, there will be less paperwork, and manufacturing
can commence at any time, as long as notice is filed fourteen
days prior to actual marketing. There are significant exclusions
and restrictions in the exemption process that are still unsatisfactory to manufacturers, however.

Exemptions to PMNs are obviously advantageous to the
chemical industry. But given the large number of new chemicals and the even larger number of PMNs, exempting certain
chemicals may be a sensible way to adjust regulatory strategy

in that it may help concentrate attention on the more dangerous chemicals. Scientists consider high molecular weight polymers to be relatively nontoxic, and EPA is following the weight of scientific judgment in exempting them from PMN scrutiny. Exempting low-volume chemicals and site-limited intermediates represents a regulatory judgment that the costs of review outweigh the risks of no review. However, in the case of exemptions, only experience can tell whether it is a good idea; but it is a sensible trial.

Evaluating the PMN system

Evaluation of the PMN system is impeded by the degree of expertise necessary to judge the scientific quality of EPA's decisions. Evaluation is even further complicated by the very high percentage of PMN submissions that omit significant information because manufacturers claim confidentiality. Approximately 50 percent of PMNs contain at least one claim of confidentiality on chemical formula, name of manufacturer, intended uses, tests performed, amounts to be manufactured, or other information, and some PMNs claim that everything about the new chemical is confidential. The General Accounting Office and the Office of Technology Assessment—both exempt from the confidentiality restrictions—have begun to study the implementation of TSCA, but their reports cannot divulge any confidential information on which their conclusions may have been based.[34]

It is clear, however, that the new system already has deterred production of some new chemicals. For instance, one manufacturer withdrew a PMN notice in April 1980 and did not manufacture six new plasticizers because EPA ordered a delay on production. The agency had required the manufacturer to develop and supply additional data on the chemicals' dangers.[35] But some industry toxicologists question whether these plasticizers were more dangerous than those already on the market.

Detailed review and regulatory action against new chemicals have been relatively rare as a percentage of PMN submissions. Only eighteen (3 percent) of PMN submissions received detailed reviews in 1981; the number increased in 1982 to fifty (6.25 percent). The Office of Toxic Substances initiated eleven "unusual actions" during 1981 and thirty-one during 1982. These included: (1) suspensions of the review period to allow more time for scrutiny, (2) voluntary agreements under which manufacturers agreed to restrict the use of their new chemical in some way that EPA found sufficient to remove it from the category of unreasonable risk, and (3) formal rule-making proceedings to block manufacture of proposed new chemicals. In addition, six PMN notices were withdrawn by manufacturers in 1981 and sixteen in 1982; some of these would have been subject to enforcement action had they continued through the detailed review process.

The number of PMNs held beyond ninety days increased during 1983 and 1984. By early 1985 more than 10 percent of PMNs were being temporarily delayed. Whether this actually is a result of deeper scrutiny or is merely indicative of a backlog of work within EPA is difficult to discern. Still, only a very small number (less than 0.4 percent) have been rejected entirely on the grounds that the chemical presents an unreasonable risk. There are several possible interpretations: (1) manufacturers may be voluntarily refraining from production of the more risky new chemicals, at least in part because they expect that the substances would not be approved, (2) the original estimates that 5 to 20 percent of new chemicals would be dangerous were inaccurate, or (3) the PMN system is not screening out some of the riskier substances.

Strategies for Chemicals Already in Use

The task of monitoring some three hundred to four hundred new chemicals each year is difficult enough. But what of the sixty thousand or more existing chemicals, of which unknown thousands may have negative effects on human health or on the ecosystem. This task is staggering, and since attention can be devoted to only a relatively small number of chemicals each year, priorities must somehow be set. One way of setting priorities is by trial and error: wait for the consequences to become known and then deal with those that emerge soonest and are most severe. This strategy still is being used in Japan, Germany, and most other nations, and, as we saw in the case of pesticides, trial and error can be a viable way of setting regulatory priorities. However, TSCA attempts to improve on the results that could be achieved through such trial-and-error by imposing a priority-setting process.

TSCA established the Interagency Testing Committee (ITC) "to make recommendations to the Administrator respecting the chemical substances and mixtures to which the [EPA] Administrator should give priority consideration."[36] The committee is instructed to consider "all relevant factors," including:

Production volumes;

Quantities likely to enter the environment;

Number of individuals who will be exposed;

Similarity in structure to other dangerous chemicals.

TSCA limits the total number of chemical substances and mixtures on the list at any one time to a maximum of fifty, and gives EPA just one year to respond to each ITC recommendation. Clearly, the intent is to identify and force action on high-priority testing needs and to keep EPA from being overwhelmed by the sheer size of the evaluation task.

Structure and mechanics of the ITC

The ITC is composed of eight formal representatives and six liaison representatives from a total of fourteen federal agencies, departments, and programs. The ITC has the equivalent of a staff of about eighteen professionals, most of whom are from outside consulting organizations. The committee's budget of about $400,000 remained constant in the early 1980s as did its workload. The ITC meets once every two weeks for a full day, and most members spend additional time preparing for such meetings. But all members have heavy responsibilities in their regular agencies, so their ITC work is a

part-time activity. These conditions are not ideal for such demanding work.

By 1986 the Interagency Testing Committee had issued
eighteen semi-annual reports, naming over one hundred individual chemical substances or classes of chemicals for priority
testing. To arrive at these recommendations, the first step is a
computer search of scientific articles on toxicity, from which is
developed a working list of several thousand potentially dangerous chemicals. These chemicals then are scored on the basis
of production volume and the other criteria listed above. The
highest scoring chemicals are subjected to detailed staff review, and the ITC reaches its decisions on the basis of a ten- to
fifty-page dossier on each of approximately sixty chemicals per
year. The ITC recommends for priority testing those chemicals
that combine high exposures with probable high toxicity. In
this process, nearly four thousand chemicals were considered
by 1986, of which approximately five hundred were reviewed
in detail.

Problems to date

Testing classes of chemicals.   Many of the ITC's early
test recommendations were for broad classes of chemicals. Because there are so many chemicals that can pose dangers, the
committee hoped to speed up the testing process by focusing
on classes of chemicals rather than on individual chemicals.
But such testing requires that appropriate groupings of chemicals be identified, and this is nearly impossible. When EPA
began investigating how to pursue the ITC's recommendation
on benzidine-based dyes, for example, there proved to be
some five hundred of these dyes that were combined and marketed under a total of twenty-five thousand different trade
names. A single category simply could not encompass these
chemicals' diverse exposure expectations, production volumes,
structure-activity relationships, and other characteristics relevant to testing. A similar problem arose with priority testing of
the organic metallic compounds known as alkyltins,[37] and, as a
result, the ITC's recent testing recommendations have generally been for individual chemicals.

How many people are exposed?   One of the main criteria in setting testing priorities is the number of people likely to be exposed to a chemical. No matter how toxic, a chemical that is manufactured in small quantities and contained will not create many problems. Unfortunately, however, available information about exposure levels is minimal.

The only nearly comprehensive data base available in the mid-1980s is based on a 1972 survey of five thousand workplaces by the National Occupational Health Survey (NOHS). It relied partly on an indirect measurement method that now seems questionable. For example, because many degreasing solvents contain chlorobenzene, all employees in workplaces that used such solvents were assumed to have been exposed to this chemical. This assumption yielded estimates that are now considered by EPA to have exaggerated exposures by up to 1,000 percent.

The NOHS does not take into account chemical exposures outside the workplace, yet there is no other source of such information. Nor is there, for most chemicals, standard scientific literature on exposures. A Chemicals Inventory kept by EPA contains information on more than fifty thousand chemicals, but it is not updated to reflect current production or imports, and it was never intended as a means of calculating probable exposures. As a result, analysis of exposures is the "weakest part of our analysis—across the board" according to one of the EPA officials responsible for making decisions about priority testing.

EPA's backlog of cases.   EPA is required by TSCA to respond to the ITC's priority recommendations within twelve months of the date they are added to the list, but EPA has not always met this schedule. As of mid-1980 EPA had proposed responses to only four of the thirty-three chemicals whose one-year deadline had expired. The Natural Resources Defense Council, a prominent environmental group, brought suit against EPA in an attempt to remedy the delays, and the court ordered EPA to develop a plan for timely testing.[38] EPA complied with the order, and was fully caught up on its cases by late 1983.

Voluntary agreements with industry. EPA in 1980–81 decided to negotiate, rather than order, testing; the agency claims that it can get industry to test more quickly by this approach. Most ITC members find the arrangement acceptable, as does a study by the General Accounting Office.[39] But the Natural Resources Defense Council contends that voluntary testing is a violation of TSCA and that it weakens public protection.[40] If voluntary testing continues to work satisfactorily, approximately half of the ITC recommendations to date will have led to earlier or more in-depth testing of chemicals than would have occurred without such a priority-setting strategy.

Progress and Continuing Problems

A comprehensive analysis of U.S. policy toward toxic chemicals would necessarily examine many more issues than have been discussed in this chapter, but several conclusions are evident.

There has been a great deal of improvement in particular facets of the regulation and use of toxic chemicals as a result of trial-and-error learning. For example, Paris Green, which was once a severe threat to human health, is no longer used on fruits and vegetables. Similarly, use has been curtailed of DDT and many other persistent pesticides; current insecticides degrade into relatively nontoxic components much faster than those used in 1970, 1950, or even 1920.

Also, significant adjustments to the regulatory system are being made that should improve on trial and error. As a result of the premanufacture notification system, some offending chemicals will be screened out prior to introduction. The Interagency Testing Committee is gradually developing priority-setting procedures that should help direct governmental attention to the more dangerous chemicals and curtail use of such chemicals before problems actually arise. While TSCA is administered more laxly than environmentalists consider warranted, still, it is likely that many risky chemicals of the future will be spotted early instead of decades after their distribution throughout the economy and ecosystem.

Legal and institutional innovations have improved the ability of federal, state, and local governments to cope with toxic chemical problems, and it is a positive development that, within the past two decades, environmental protection agencies, major environmental statutes, and environmental groups have come into existence in most industrial nations.

However, these optimistic conclusions must be tempered by four qualifications. First, since there is a twenty- to thirty-year delay between exposure to carcinogens and manifestation of cancer, we have not yet witnessed the results of chemicals used during the past several decades. Moreover, there were approximately ten times as many synthetic chemicals produced between 1965 and 1985 as in all previous human history. While the trends do not indicate an imminent cancer epidemic, we must wait for more time to pass before assessing the toll on human health.

Another qualification concerns priority setting. The effort made to set priorities is noteworthy—a genuine breakthrough in government's approach to regulation. To date, however, success has been limited. While responsible agencies are becoming more proficient at the task of setting priorities, it is too early to tell whether the results of these efforts will be significant.

Third, we have emphasized repeatedly that a central part of trial-and-error learning is the recognition of negative feedback. However, the PMN system is partially insulated from such feedback because of the confidentiality guaranteed to chemical manufacturers. This may be a predicament with no satisfactory resolution. Forcing manufacturers to reveal trade secrets would reduce their incentive to innovate and would increase their incentive to circumvent the system.

Finally, considerable—perhaps excessive—faith in science was displayed by Congress and by environmentalists who argued for premarket screening of new chemicals. The ability to make intelligent advance judgments about a new chemical depends partly on the results of tests for toxicity. But just as important are how a chemical will be used and the quantities in which it will be manufactured. PMN notices give the original manufacturer's estimate on these matters, but the uses to which a chemical is put can change. So the assignment given

EPA is as much a requirement for guesswork on a new chemical's commercial future as it is for scientific testing of the chemical's dangers. Fortunately, TSCA established another regulatory process to monitor chemicals that are being put to significant new uses; but that regulatory process is even less proven than the PMN system.[41]

Our conclusion is that, overall, scientific analysis has not entirely replaced trial and error in the regulation of toxic chemicals.

3

Nuclear Power

Of all modern technologies, the one most closely associated in the public's mind with potential catastrophe is nuclear power. If a substantial portion of the radioactive material contained in a reactor were released to the atmosphere, the results could be disastrous. No one on either side of the nuclear debate denies this; what each argues about is the likelihood of a serious accident and the magnitude of its effects.[1]

The potential hazard from nuclear power is very different from that posed by use of toxic chemicals. With the exception of manufacturing accidents or extraordinarily careless disposal of chemical wastes, damage from chemicals typically is dispersed and, at worst, would result in a large number of individual illnesses and deaths spread out over space and time. In contrast, a nuclear catastrophe can result from a single, large accident. Because nuclear consequences are so severe, regulators cannot use the same trial-and-error strategies they employ for toxic chemical control. Nor can they rely on advance testing, because the large-scale nature of the hazard makes a definitive, controlled study of a nuclear accident impractical. And short of prohibiting the construction of a nuclear power plant, there is no equivalent to the strategy of screening out particularly risky chemicals.

This chapter examines the strategies developed by regulators of nuclear power in their attempts to cope with this more concentrated type of catastrophe.

The Emergence of Reactor Safety Strategies

The early land-based reactors

In 1947 the Atomic Energy Commission (AEC) estab-lished a Reactor Safeguards Committee (RSC) comprised of leading atomic scientists from outside AEC; the first chairman was Edward Teller.[2] The committee's function, as its name implies, was to determine whether the reactors then being planned by the AEC could be built without endangering public safety. As its basic approach to reactor safety, the committee decided to continue the practice established by the Manhattan Project during World War II (that is, the effort to develop the atomic bomb) of keeping reactors isolated from the population as much as possible. Thus, if a serious release of radioactivity did occur, the effects on public safety would be minimized. Each reactor was to be surrounded by two concentric areas. The inner area would be unpopulated and under the complete control of the AEC, and the outer area would be populated by no more than ten thousand people. The size of the two areas depended partly on the powerfulness of the reactor: the greater the power, the larger the areas. The size of the outer area also depended on the type of reactor and on the meteo-rology, hydrology, and seismology of the geographical region.[3]

The first test of this safety plan occurred in 1946–47 and involved a reactor designed to test materials used in more advanced reactors. The materials testing reactor was relatively large for its day, although it is about one-tenth the size of current reactors. The AEC originally planned to construct this reactor at Argonne National Laboratory just outside Chicago, where it would be accessible to scientists at the lab. However, the Reactor Safeguards Committee ruled that the reactor was too large to be built so close to a city. Either the reactor would have to be redesigned and scaled down in power, or it would have to be moved to a less populated site.

The director of the lab, who might have been expected to fight for this project, instead endorsed removal to a remote site as a reasonable policy: "For a nation with the land space of ours and with the financial resources of ours, adopting a very conservative attitude on safety is not an unnecessary luxury."[4] In fact, he proposed the establishment of a very remote site where all the early versions of reactors could be tested. This proposal was "most enthusiastically" endorsed by the Reactor Safeguards Committee and approved by the AEC in May 1949.[5] The site was in a barren desert section of Idaho about forty miles from Idaho Falls, then a city of twenty thousand.[6]

Most early nuclear reactors were built at the Idaho test station. The only major exception was a reactor then under development by General Electric at its Knolls Atomic Power Lab (KAPL) outside Schenectady, New York. Although this reactor was as powerful as the materials testing reactor, the scientists at KAPL proposed to build it at a site near Knolls, which was about ten miles away from any heavily populated areas. Given the size of the reactor, this proposal caused some concern among the Reactor Safeguards Committee. On the other hand, building the reactor in Idaho might have prevented the Knolls personnel from continuing their reactor research. The committee feared that this "would be disastrous to the leadership of the United States in atomic energy." So the RSC in fall 1947 "concluded unenthusiastically that a location near Schenectady might be acceptable."[7]

In response to the RSC's concerns, plans for the KAPL reactor changed significantly. Scientists at the laboratory developed new ways to ensure that public exposure would be minimized in the event of a serious release of radioactivity. They proposed that the entire reactor facility be enclosed in a gas-tight steel sphere. The sphere would be designed to withstand "a disruptive core explosion from nuclear energy release, followed by sodium-water and air reactions."[8] It would thus contain within the reactor facility "any radioactivity that might be produced in a reactor accident."[9] The AEC accepted this proposal, which thereafter became a major safety component in all civilian nuclear power plant construction. Moreover, the Knolls reactor was still to be built in a relatively unpopulated area; containment was not considered a complete substitute for remote siting.

In its early years the RSC made a number of less crucial

safety decisions. In approving a small reactor for Argonne National Lab, for example, the committee required that the amount of plutonium and radioactive waste generated in the reactor be strictly limited. In evaluating this reactor as well as the one at Knolls, the RSC considered not only the risk of accidents but also the potential for sabotage. In addition, the committee discussed in a preliminary way a variety of other safeguards, including emergency arrangements for cooling a reactor by flooding and other automatic safety devices.[10]

The important point is that by the early 1950s, a general strategy for coping with the potential for catastrophe had emerged. Reactors were to be built on very remote sites or on relatively remote sites with containment. Decision makers believed that this policy would substantially protect the public should a serious reactor accident occur.

The early submarine reactors

At about the same time that this safety strategy was evolving, the first nuclear submarine reactors were being developed. The earliest models were built at remote test sites on land, and the reactors that were actually used in submarines were constructed soon after these land-based versions.[11] Unfortunately, the strategies used in protecting against serious accidents with land-based reactors were not applicable to submarine reactors: "Since the sixty-man submarine crew had no avenue of escape while the ship was at sea and major ports were generally large population centers, remote siting could not be relied upon to acceptably limit the consequences of an accident. Nor could containment be reasonably engineered for a submarine."[12]

This led scientists and engineers to devise an entirely different approach: rather than attempt to contain or isolate the effects of accidents, they attempted to prevent accidents, and they employed a variety of tactics toward this end. While most of these tactics consisted of applying unusually stringent standards to such procedures as operator training, program auditing, and quality control, two of the tactics—designing with wide margins for error and with redundancies—were less common to industrial practices and were devised to reduce the probability of serious nuclear accidents.[13]

The components and systems of most machines—those of a car, for instance—are built to withstand the average or likely set of operating conditions. But submarine reactors were built to withstand "the worst credible set of circumstances, rather than . . . average or probable conditions."[14] Each of the components was constructed of materials that could withstand substantially higher than likely temperatures and pressures, and each of the systems was designed to operate for substantially longer periods of time than necessary.

Not only were the components and systems built to withstand extreme conditions, but also redundancies were included in the design to serve as back ups in case systems or components did fail.[15] Each safety-related function of the reactor could be performed by more than one component or system. For example, if one system for injecting the control rods into the core failed, another independent system could be used, or if a primary set of pumps failed to operate, a back-up set could be put into operation.

For land-based reactors, then, the early strategy was to isolate and contain the effects of accidents. For sea-based reactors, the strategy was to prevent accidents altogether.

Prevention Plus Containment: Safety in Early Commercial Reactors

By the late 1950s the AEC required that both prevention and containment strategies be applied to land-based nuclear reactors. The prevention strategy followed more or less the same pattern used for submarine reactors—systems were conservatively designed with wide margins for error and redundancies.[16] For instance, the material that sheathed the reactor fuel had to withstand higher temperatures and more corrosive conditions than were likely, and the pressure vessel (which contained the reactor core) and the coolant pipes were built to withstand much higher than expected pressures and temperatures.

Reactors also were designed so that if any safety-related component or system failed, a back-up component or system would perform the necessary function. Each reactor was required to have two independent off-site sources of electrical power with completely independent transmission lines capable of providing all the power required to run the plant. Further, more than one method had to be provided for injecting control rods into the core, several coolant loops had to be passed through the core (so that if one failed, the others would still be available), and back-up pumps and valves had to be provided.

The AEC also required that reactors be equipped with emergency safety systems; this constituted an additional level of redundancy. Engineers attempted to anticipate malfunctions and sequences of malfunctions that might lead to serious releases of radioactivity, and they then designed emergency systems that would operate when such malfunctions occurred. For example, if one or more coolant pipes ruptured and too little coolant reached the core, the fuel might melt and radioactivity could be released. To counteract this possibility, all reactors were required to be equipped with "emergency core cooling systems," which consisted of alternate sources of water (coolant) that could be sprayed or pumped into the core if the coolant level fell too low.[17]

In spite of these preventive measures, the AEC recognized that serious accidents might still occur, so it also required that measures be taken to protect humans and the environment from the effects of possible nuclear accidents. The early method for accomplishing such protection was to build reactors away from populated areas. By the end of the 1950s, however, the AEC began to modify this approach. Over time, reactor sites that had been initially remote were becoming populated, and there were few remote sites in areas where nuclear power would be most commercially viable. In addition, remote siting involved increasingly expensive power transmission costs. Largely in response to growing pressure from the nuclear industry, the AEC evolved a new policy that shifted the reliance on remote siting to a combination of siting and containment safeguards: the less remote the site, the more extensive the other required safeguards.[18] By the late 1950s it was required that all reactors be designed with containment.[19] The AEC stipulated that the reactor's containment building be strong enough to withstand "the pressures and temperatures associated with the largest credible energy release" arising from a reactor accident and be almost gas-tight so that only very small amounts of radioactivity could leak into the atmosphere.[20]

To determine whether the containment system proposed for a reactor was adequate, the AEC attempted to determine whether it could withstand the "maximum credible accident." There are many conceivable sequences of events that can lead to a release of fission products. Some, such as failure of the pressure vessel in which the core is located, were considered incredible, and these were eliminated from consideration. Remaining sequences of events were considered credible, and the maximum credible accident, as its name suggests, was the most severe of these events.

For the light water reactors used in the United States, two ways such an accident could occur were envisioned. One was "an inadvertent insertion of reactivity [such as an increase in rate of chain reaction] leading to fuel damage and rupture of the primary coolant line," and a second was "brittle shear [a sudden break] of a primary coolant line with subsequent failure of the emergency cooling system."[21] Once the maximum credible accident had been specified, the AEC calculated the most extreme consequences of this accident. On this basis, the AEC screened applications for nuclear reactor licenses, requiring that the design submitted be sufficient to prevent radiation from reaching the public in the event of such a maximum credible accident.[22]

The underlying assumption of the AEC in setting forth its two-pronged safety strategy of the 1950s and early 1960s was that errors in reactor design, construction, and operation would in fact occur. As much as nuclear regulators sought to eliminate error, they never believed that this could be achieved; the uncertainties and complexity associated with nuclear technology are too great. The basic premise of reactor design was to make reactors not free of errors but forgiving of them. Thus, reactors were built on the assumption that at some point, critical components would fail, temperatures and pressures would rise higher than expected, safety systems and back-up safety systems would fail, and even the emergency safety systems might fail. Reactors were to be built to withstand such circumstances.

The Revised Strategy: Emphasizing Prevention

The AEC modified its approach to reactor safety in 1966–67 when the size of reactors sharply increased and doubts emerged as to whether containment would withstand a maximum credible accident. The largest reactor in operation in the early 1960s produced two hundred megawatts of electricity, but, beginning in 1963, orders began to be placed for much more powerful reactors. Three reactors ordered in this year were two to three times more powerful than any reactor then in operation. Seven ordered in 1965 were three to five times more powerful, and twenty-one ordered in 1966 were six times more powerful. This increase in reactor power had a crucial impact on the AEC's safety strategy.[23] If the coolant were lost in one of the large reactors and the emergency cooling system failed, a breach of containment and an escape of fission products into the environment might possibly occur. For example, the reactor core might melt into a molten mass, which in turn might melt through the reactor vessel, fall to the floor of the containment building and melt through that as well. (This scenario came to be known as the "China Syndrome.")[24]

Failure of containment was not inevitable in the event of a core melt; even in large reactors, the containment shields were strong enough to withstand many of the possible effects. But as reactor size increased, containment could no longer be fully relied upon to withstand the most serious possible effects.

The AEC responded to this situation by reviewing ways to reinforce containment. One manufacturer proposed a core catcher, a water-cooled, stainless steel device placed below the reactor vessel that presumably would catch the reactor core if it melted through the reactor vessel.[25] Other possibilities included larger containment vessels, dual or triple containment shields, and systems for venting or igniting accumulated hydrogen, but none of these devices could ensure containment of the worst credible effects of core melts. The behavior of melted reactor cores was unknown. Furthermore, the range of possible consequences of a core melt was sufficiently broad that no single device could cover all the possibilities. For example, a core catcher might help if the core melted through the vessel, but it would be of little help in the event of a dangerous buildup of pressure.

Most observers concluded that no practical system could be devised for guaranteeing containment in the event of a serious core melt in a large reactor. Core catchers and similar devices might reduce the probability that containment would fail, but they could not make the probability low enough for the AEC to continue to rely on containment as the primary defense. The AEC had to modify its strategy.

Therefore, in 1967 the AEC decided to emphasize its prevention strategy.[26] If it could no longer guarantee containment of fission products released by core melts in large reactors, the AEC would attempt to prevent the fission products from being released in the first place.[27] This meant the inclusion of wider margins for error, more redundancies, and enhanced emergency safety systems. The change was one of degree: the larger reactors were to be designed even more conservatively than the smaller ones.

This increase in conservative design is illustrated by changes made in the requirements for emergency core cooling systems. Emergency cooling systems previously were designed to handle only relatively small leaks or breaks in the normal cooling system. In 1966, the capacity of these systems was substantially increased, and the new systems were designed to protect against the largest and most severe possible primary coolant system pipe breaks. In addition, since a large break would be accompanied by a violent release of steam that might hurl missiles of ruptured pipe, measures were taken to protect vulnerable components of the emergency systems.[28]

Redundancies were added to the system as well. Pressurized light water reactors now would have independent systems for emergency cooling. One system was passive and consisted of several very large tanks of water. If one of the large primary cooling pipes were to break, the pressure in the core would decrease below the pressure in the water tanks and the tanks would open and "rapidly discharge a large volume of water . . . into the reactor vessel and core."[29] Emergency cooling also was provided via an injection system for pumping water into the core. Both high- and low-pressure pumps were available for different types of pipe breaks, and each pump had its own back up.[30] Thus, the emergency core cooling system, which itself constituted a second level of redundancy, was comprised of two systems, each of which was redundantly designed.[31]

The shift toward greater reliance on prevention did not represent a change in the AEC's underlying approach: the AEC's goal was still to make reactors forgiving of errors. However, the increased emphasis on prevention did make the regulatory process considerably more complicated. As long as containment was considered to be guaranteed, the main issue in the regulatory process was whether the particular containment system and site proposed for a new reactor would withstand the worst credible effects of the worst (or maximum) credible accident. There might be disagreement over the definition of credible accidents and over the maximum amount of their effects, but at least the range of possible issues open to debate was relatively restricted.

The shift in emphasis to prevention opened up a much larger set of debatable issues. In order to prevent radiation releases, regulators had to anticipate not only the worst effects of accidents but also all the credible potential causes. Included in these causes were failures in the coolant system, the electrical system, the control system, and so on; the emergency systems had to prevent these failures from triggering serious accidents. Nuclear power regulators needed to anticipate the variety of reactor conditions that might arise as a result of the many possible failures, the emergency systems responses to these conditions, and the consequences of those responses.

For example, in order to ensure that the emergency cooling system was capable of cooling the reactor core in the event of a double-ended break in the largest cooling pipe, estimates had to be made of the following conditions, among others:

Distribution of temperatures in the core after such a break;

Effects on the core of a loss of coolant;

Effects of violent releases of steam from the core as coolant is injected into the core;

Possible reactions of the fuel cladding (the metal in which the fuel is sheathed) with water and steam in the core after the loss of coolant;

The rate at which emergency coolant should be injected into the core.

Some of these conditions were virtually impossible to calculate without actual experimental meltdowns; estimating other conditions was time consuming and subject to a range of professional judgment. Requiring regulators to base safety policies on calculations of these conditions resulted in a more complex and difficult regulatory process. Debates about possible causes of serious accidents and reliability of safety systems arose. What if the pressure vessel failed? What if the emergency core cooling system did not flood the core as quickly as anticipated? What if, through some unanticipated interconnection, several supposedly independent safety systems failed simultaneously? What if the operating temperature rose and both the control rods and the pumps that circulate coolant into the reactor failed? What if the turbine failed and pieces of it were hurled off like missiles? What if pipes cracked as a result of stress corrosion?

Such questions could go on endlessly; reactors are so complex that it was always possible to postulate some new combination of events that conceivably could trigger a core melt and a nuclear accident. Since the emphasis had shifted to prevention, prediction of all such combinations of events was critical to reactor safety, and newly suggested combinations of events, while remote, were not something regulators could afford to rule out. Furthermore, there was no way to dispel lingering doubts about whether all the possible triggering events had been anticipated, whether the capacities of the emergency systems had been estimated accurately, and whether all the ways emergency systems might fail had been examined. Both in practice and in principle, it was impossible to prove that the unexpected would not occur, and so the debates went on.

This open-ended regulatory process may or may not produce added safety gains, but it has proven extraordinarily costly to the nuclear industry. The Nuclear Regulatory Commission (NRC) has ordered repeated modifications of design requirements, both for reactors under construction and for those already in operation, and these modifications have contributed substantially to sharp increases in the capital costs of reactors. As early as 1974, an Atomic Energy Commission study estimated that "reactors scheduled for service in the early 1970s required about 3.5 man-hours/KWe [kilowatt-electric] to construct, whereas those scheduled for service in the early 1980s would require 8.5 man-hours/KWe."[32] A 1979 study by the Departments of Energy and Labor concluded that this trend would continue, and that by the mid-1980s reactor construction would require between 13 and 18 man-hours/KWe.[33] These increases were due in part to reactor design changes intended to further reduce the probability of accidents.

The nuclear industry and critics of the regulatory process argue that many of these costly design changes do not improve safety. In their view, reactors were already safe enough in the 1970s—considerably safer than other publicly accepted structures such as large dams, chemical plants, and airports in populated areas. Why, the critics ask, should increasingly unlikely potential causes of accidents be taken into account when the probabilities of serious accidents are already minute? Why make reactors more forgiving of errors when they were already forgiving enough? The inevitable answer is that it is impossible to be sure that reactors are forgiving enough. What if all the important causes of accidents have not been anticipated? What if the capacity of an emergency system has been overestimated? What if safety systems assumed to be independent and redundant in fact are not? What if . . . ?

The Three Mile Island Accident

The debates triggered by the emphasis on prevention were brought to a head by the Three Mile Island (TMI) accident. The reactor at Three Mile Island is a pressurized water reactor. As shown in Figure 1, this type of reactor is comprised of two loops of circulating water. In the primary loop, water circulates through the reactor core, where it is heated. (It does not boil because it is at very high pressure.) From the core, it is pumped to the steam generator, and from there it passes (via tubes) through cooler, lower pressure water and causes this water to boil. The water then circulates back to the core, where it is reheated. The lower pressure water in the steam generator is in the second of the two loops. As it is boiled by the hotter water from the primary loop, it turns into steam, which then is circulated to the turbines (steam runs the turbines which generate electricity for public use). After passing through the turbines, the steam is condensed into water and pumped back into the steam generator, where the cycle repeats.

The Three Mile Island accident occurred in March 1979 and began when maintenance personnel inadvertently shut off water to the secondary loop. This began a series of normal safety measures:

1. The loop's water pump and the turbine automatically shut down (not an uncommon event);
2. This triggered an automatic shutdown of the chain reaction in the reactor (also an unremarkable event).

Even though the chain reaction ended, the decay of fission products in the reactor core continued to give off heat (as it always does). So, to remove heat from the reactor core,

3. A backup pump went into operation to circulate water in the secondary loop; and
4. A pressure relief valve opened in the primary loop (a standard measure to prevent overpressurization).

Figure 1. The pressurized water reactor

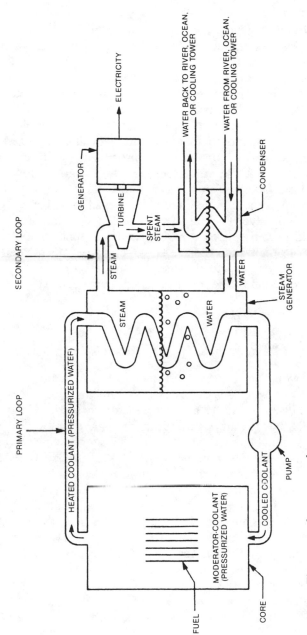

NOTE: Figure not drawn to scale.

Ordinarily, these steps would have taken care of the problem. The primary loop, which was still operating, would have brought water heated by the decay of fission products to the steam generator; the water in the secondary loop, circulated by the back-up pump, would have removed the heat. The reactor would have been restarted after a brief shutdown.

But another error occurred. The pressure relief valve, which was supposed to close automatically, remained open. Even worse, the control room instruments indicated to plant operators that the valve had closed—a fourth error. At this point serious problems began. Since the valve stayed open, pressure in the loop fell and water began to boil away through the open valve. If enough water boiled away, the reactor fuel would become exposed and parts of the fuel assembly would begin to melt and oxidize. The open valve thus created a real threat of damage to the fuel and release of fission products.

In reaction to the loss of coolant and pressure,

5. An emergency cooling system was automatically activated to replace the water that had boiled away and escaped through the valve.

This would have prevented further difficulty, but then a fifth error occurred. Misled by the instruments into thinking that the valve was closed and the reactor pressurized and full of water, the operators turned off the emergency water supply! They thought there was too much water in the reactor and actually began to remove water. All the while, water continued to escape and pressure continued to fall. By now, a considerable amount of steam had accumulated in the primary loop, making the pumps still in operation begin to vibrate, so the operators turned off these pumps. This sixth error further reduced the heat removal capacity of the system (since the circulation of the primary loop had been removing at least some of the heat from the core).

It was not until over two hours after the accident began that the operators finally realized that the valve was in fact open and that there was too little, not too much, water in the core. They then shut the valve and flooded the core with emergency coolant. But by this time, water covering a portion of the fuel had boiled away. The zirconium alloy (which sheathes the actual fuel) and other materials in the fuel assembly melted and oxidized, becoming quite brittle. Some of the fuel itself appears to have melted, but there is debate on this point. (Uranium oxide, a ceramic, has a very high melting point, so it can withstand a loss of coolant longer than other parts of the fuel assembly.) What is clear, however, is that when the embrittled fuel assembly finally was flooded again, a large segment of the core shattered and a substantial quantity of fission products were released. Most of these, however, were trapped by the containment building, as nuclear designers had planned.

Implications for regulatory strategies

The TMI accident is generally considered the worst mishap in the history of the U.S. nuclear industry. As such, it provided a good test of how forgiving nuclear reactors are. Yet the implications of the accident are ambiguous.

On the one hand, it certainly demonstrated that reactors are forgiving of errors. Maintenance errors touched off the incident, and the stuck pressure relief valve helped turn this occurrence into a major emergency. There were operator errors during the accident—shutting down the emergency cooling system, removing water from the primary loop, and shutting down the pumps in the primary loop. And there was an error in the original design—the instrumentation that led operators to believe the reactor was full of water when it was not. Despite all these errors, emergency systems were still available to prevent more serious consequences.

Moreover, the health consequences of the accident have been judged about as severe as a car accident. In the words of the Kemeny Commission (appointed by President Carter to investigate the accident), the levels of radioactivity released in the accident "will have a negligible effect on the physical health" of the population.[34] Furthermore, according to widely accepted analyses performed by several groups, even if the accident had continued until the core had melted through the reactor vessel and the containment floor (the "China Syndrome"), the consequences still would not have been severe. The Kemeny Commission reported that: "even if a meltdown had occurred, there is a high probability that the containment building and the hard rock on which the TMI-2 containment building is built would have been able to prevent the escape of a large amount of radioactivity."[35] That is to say, containment probably would not have failed.

The analyses also show that the TMI accident probably would not have continued long enough for a complete meltdown. The stuck valve through which water was escaping remained undetected for over two hours, but it would have taken "dozens of hours" for the fuel to melt through the reactor vessel and containment floor. Throughout that time, "restoration of water . . . by any means, with or without closure of the [stuck] relief valve would [have] stop[ped] progress of the damage or melting."[36] Water could have been restored by a variety of independent mechanisms provided by the conservative reactor design. These included a high pressure water injection system, a core flooding system, a containment spray, and containment coolers.[37] And despite the fact that the operators failed to assess the problem for over two hours, they would have had "many more 'observables' available to them had the accident progressed further."[38] That is, if the accident had continued, there would have been many indications that the core was melting and that it therefore should be flooded. So the accident appears to have demonstrated that reactors are extremely forgiving of errors, as the AEC and NRC had planned.

On the other hand, the accident called into serious question the safety strategy based on prevention. By the 1970s core melts and containment of their effects no longer were even considered in the reactor licensing process because nuclear regulators assumed that meltdowns would be prevented. Yet at Three Mile Island, part of the core seems to have melted and fission products were released. This supported the argument made by those skeptical of the prevention strategy. To prevent errors from triggering core melts, all credible sequences of events leading to melts must be anticipated. Yet the sequence of the TMI accident had not been foreseen. How were regulators to know in the future whether all possible accident sequences had been anticipated?

The TMI accident inspired a series of reviews of the nuclear regulatory system by Congress, the Nuclear Regulatory Commission, the nuclear industry, and the state of Pennsylvania, as well as the independent, President-appointed Kemeny Commission. The reviews recommended a variety of changes and emphasized two potential causes of core melts that had heretofore received insufficient attention. One of these causes was operator error; prior to the TMI accident, regulators had directed most attention to design errors rather than operator errors. Minor malfunctions, such as stuck valves, also had been underemphasized. Attention had been focused on relatively improbable, severe malfunctions, such as a two-sided break in the largest cooling pipe. Regulators had assumed that if reactors were designed to prevent serious malfunctions, this would also prevent less serious malfunctions.

Because the TMI accident demonstrated that even minor malfunctions and operator errors could lead to core melts, it was necessary that the potential for such errors be examined more carefully in future reactor design and regulation. These recommendations were consistent with the pre-TMI strategy of prevention and thus generated little opposition.

A second set of recommendations was more controversial. It included proposals for a return to remote siting, systems for filtering and venting gas that might build up in the containment during a core melt, core catchers, emergency evacuation procedures, and distribution to the nearby population of potassium iodide pills to counteract the effects of radioactive iodine that might be released into the environment by a core melt. Each of these measures was intended to contain or otherwise mitigate the effects of core melts—a step that many postaccident reviews deemed necessary because a portion of the core was damaged in the TMI accident.

The NRC did not expect these new containment measures to perform the same function as the containment strategy of the late 1950s and early 1960s. The earlier approach was based on the expectation that containment would withstand the effects of serious core melts; no such assumption was made after

TMI. For large contemporary reactors, there still could be no guarantee that containment could withstand a core melt. At best, the proposed measures would reduce the probability that radiation released in a core melt would escape into the environment. Vented containment and core catchers would reduce the probability that containment would fail; remote siting and emergency planning would reduce the probability that large numbers of people would be exposed to escaped radiation if containment failed; potassium iodide pills would reduce the probability that people exposed to radiation would develop cancer of the thyroid.

The fact that these recommended containment measures could not entirely prevent serious public exposures to radiation made them vulnerable to the same problems that plagued earlier prevention efforts. If the probability that core melts would lead to public radiation exposure was to be reduced, when would it be sufficiently reduced? Reactor systems are so complex that there might always be additional design changes that would further reduce the probability of a core melt. In the event of a meltdown, would the preparation of emergency evacuation plans be sufficient? Or would it be necessary to have emergency evacuation plans as well as remote siting plus systems for venting containment? Or would all of these be necessary plus core catchers, larger containments, and smaller reactors? Furthermore, serious doubt existed among some observers about whether any of these changes were really necessary. The changes were being proposed in the wake of an accident that had demonstrated the forgiving nature of reactors. Perhaps reactors were already safe enough. If not, when would they be?

The nuclear community has been struggling with this issue for over a decade, and it seems no closer to a resolution now than it was originally. As will be discussed in detail in the concluding chapter, there was a significant effort in the early 1980s to establish a safety goal—a point at which reactors would be deemed safe enough. Such a goal was established, but it did not resolve the difficulties. Ironically, this effort fell victim to the same uncertainties that created the need for a safety goal in the first place: even if agreement could be reached on an acceptable level of risk, how would regulators know that a given reactor had achieved that level? How could they be sure that they had correctly anticipated all the significant possibilities leading to an accident?

Conclusion: From One Dilemma to Another

At the outset of the nuclear era, the combination of high uncertainty and potential for catastrophe created a serious dilemma for nuclear regulators. They were confronted with a technology so complex that errors in reactor design, construction, and operation were virtually certain to occur. At the same time, they were confronted with the possibility that such errors could lead to intolerable consequences. The regulators overcame this dilemma by requiring that reactors be forgiving of errors. If errors in design, construction, and operation were inevitable, then the best that could be done was to require that reactors be designed so as to make it unlikely that the errors would actually lead to the intolerable consequences.

Unfortunately, in overcoming this first dilemma, regulators created a new and perhaps more intractable dilemma: how forgiving of errors should reactors be? The technology is so complex that there is always one more method possible for reducing the likelihood that an error will trigger serious consequences and one more sequence of events that conceivably could lead to these consequences. So how safe is safe enough?

The pointedness of this question for nuclear power helps in understanding the dilemma of toxic chemicals regulation. In both cases, regulators were confronted by uncertainty combined with a potential for catastrophe. In both cases, regulators confronted the dilemma and devised deliberate strategies for coping with it. The strategies were quite different, which in itself is a measure of the intelligence of the process: regulators were adapting their strategies to the differences in the problems they faced. And in both cases, in an attempt to overcome the first dilemma, regulators discovered a new dilemma: when had their efforts gone far enough?

In setting priorities for toxic chemicals regulation, why focus on the top fifty chemicals? Why not sixty, or one hundred? When conducting premanufacture screening for new chemicals, how toxic must a chemical be to necessitate restrictions or outright prohibition? Now that new techniques can detect chemical traces at the parts per billion or trillion level and questionable chemicals can be detected throughout the environment and in many consumer products, how much of a toxic substance is acceptable? This is precisely the same problem faced by the nuclear regulators as they realize that containment can no longer be guaranteed. What level of risk is acceptable? And how can regulators be sure that that level has in fact been achieved?

We explore this problem in the concluding chapter. For the moment, suffice it to say that no satisfactory strategy has yet emerged to address this new dilemma.

4

Recombinant
DNA Research

In May 1984 Federal District Judge John Sirica delayed an outdoor experiment that would have tested a genetically engineered organism developed to protect crops against frost damage. This decision was the most visible expression to that date of public concern about regulating environmental risks created by the biotechnology industry. But the attention directed at biotechnological risks during the mid-1980s was mild compared to the alarm these risks caused a decade earlier. At that time genetic engineering seemed headed for the same regulatory fate as nuclear power.

In the mid-1970s the risks associated with splicing genes from one organism into another through recombinant DNA (rDNA) techniques were causing widespread concern in the scientific community. Public fears of rDNA research, fueled by the possibility of a catastrophic release of dangerous organisms into the environment, were remarkably similar to fears about nuclear power.[1] Interest groups led by dissident scientists gained widespread visibility, media coverage became increasingly sensational, and local controversies raged in towns where universities proposed conducting rDNA research. Congress was close to passing legislation that would have created a new regulatory agency, patterned on the Nuclear Regulatory Commission, to oversee rDNA research.

By the early 1980s, however, the furor surrounding rDNA

research had all but vanished. The regulations that seemed so imminent in 1977 never materialized. Congress failed to pass a single regulatory measure, and most local governments followed in the same path. The federal regulations imposed by the National Institutes of Health (NIH) prior to 1977 were progressively relaxed, and the complete abolition of these regulations was seriously considered (but rejected) in 1982. Where media had initially emphasized risks of the research, now it focused on the future benefits and the exciting prospects of the biotechnology industry. This unexpected course of the recombinant DNA debate was at least in part the result of the strategies employed in diagnosing and preventing anticipated rDNA research-related catastrophes. This chapter examines those strategies.

Stages of the Controversy

In 1971 the Stanford biochemist Paul Berg proposed to insert DNA from SV40, a virus that can cause tumors in lower animals, into a common type of bacterium that inhabits the human intestine. Berg's proposal, which would have been the first recombinant DNA experiment, triggered concern about the risks of such research. Suppose, some of Berg's colleagues hypothesized, the recombined genes could initiate tumor growth in humans, and suppose a lab worker were accidently infected with them? It was possible that an epidemic of an unknown disease might thereby be created. These scientists believed that a closer examination of risks should precede such an experiment.

In deference to his colleagues, Berg canceled the experiment, but the doubts raised about it and similar experiments did not abate. Concern in the scientific community continued to increase until June 1973, when participants at the Gordon Research Conference on Nucleic Acids formally requested that the National Academy of Sciences appoint a committee to examine the risks of rDNA research. A committee was formed, and in July 1974 it announced its recommendations in a letter published simultaneously in *Science* and *Nature*, journals that are widely read in the scientific community. The committee recommended that: (1) certain types of recombinant DNA experiments that seemed especially hazardous should be deferred until the risks were better understood, (2) the National Institutes of Health should appoint a committee to evaluate the possible risks and establish research guidelines and procedures, and (3) an international conference on the potential risks should be held. All three recommendations were carried out. Scientists voluntarily observed a moratorium on the specified types of experiments, the NIH established what became known as the Recombinant DNA Advisory Committee to assess risks and establish research guidelines, and an international conference on rDNA research was held at Asilomar, California, in February 1975.

The conference at Asilomar is considered a landmark in the history of the rDNA controversy. After four days of meetings, the participants concluded that the moratorium on especially risky experiments should continue and that all other experiments should be performed according to safety guidelines that were set forth at the conference. The guidelines were elaborated and refined by the Recombinant DNA Advisory Committee, and in June 1976 they were formally promulgated by the NIH.[2] The guidelines prohibited six types of experiments, classified all other experiments according to degree of possible hazard, and required varying degrees of containment for each of these classes of experiments. The more potentially hazardous the experiment, the more extensive the containment requirements.

Just as the scientific community was reaching agreement on how to handle the risks of these experiments, public controversy erupted. It began at the local level in university towns throughout the United States. The most notorious local dispute took place in Cambridge, Massachusetts, in the summer of 1976. At issue was whether an old biology building should be modified to meet the containment standards required by the NIH for relatively risky rDNA experiments.[3] Disagreement within the Harvard biology department grew into a campus-wide debate. Among the leaders of the opposition to the proposed rDNA lab were Nobel laureate George Wald and his wife Ruth Hubbard, a group known as Science for the People, and several environmental groups that had been active in the debate over nuclear power. Cambridge's mayor Al Velluchi, long at odds with Harvard, led the opposition and stated its case in this way:

> We want to be damn sure the people of Cambridge won't be affected by anything that would crawl out of the laboratory. . . . It is my responsibility to investigate the danger of infections to humans. They may come up with a disease that can't be cured—even a monster. Is this the answer to Dr. Frankenstein's dream?[4]

The controversy spread throughout the country, though rarely with the intensity reached in Cambridge. By 1977 the risks of rDNA research had been debated at the local level in Ann Arbor, Bloomington, Berkeley, Madison, and San Diego and at the state level in New York, California, and New Jersey. The debates resulted in extensive media coverage, much of it sensational: "Science That Frightens Scientists" (*Atlantic*); "Creating New Forms of Life—Blessing or Curse?" (*U.S. News and World Report*); "New Strains of Life or Death?" (*New York Times Magazine*). With the media interest came a flurry of books: *Recombinant DNA, The Untold Story; Biohazard; Playing God.*[5] During 1977 alone sixteen bills for regulating rDNA research were proposed in Congress and twenty-five hearings were held. The primary bills that finally emerged in both the House and Senate called for extensive federal regulations. Senator Kennedy's bill, which was passed by the Senate Committee on Human Resources, proposed a national regulatory commission empowered to promulgate safety regulations, license and inspect facilities, and fine violators.

Kennedy's proposed national regulatory commission was reminiscent of the Nuclear Regulatory Commission; by 1977 the controversy had all the earmarks of the nuclear power debate—aroused citizenry, media sensationalism, congressional concern, and vocal opposition by dissident scientists and environmental groups. Nowhere was the intensity of the controversy and its similarity to the nuclear debate more striking than at a National Academy of Sciences meeting held in Washington D.C. in March 1977. The opening session was dominated by protesters. In front of TV cameras, they chanted, waved banners, demanded that the conference be "opened up to the people," and asserted:

> This is just the first protest. . . . We are just the little ruffling wind before the storm of public outrage. . . . This is the most important social issue of the coming next decade. . . . We are not going to go quietly. We have means at our command to resist the change in the human species. We will not go gentle [sic] into the brave new world, that new order of the ages that is being offered to us here.[6]

But the promised "storm of public outrage" and the new regulatory regime never materialized. Recombinant DNA research, unlike nuclear power, quickly receded as an issue of contention. In Congress not one of the sixteen bills on rDNA research proposed in 1977 ever reached the floor. Only two bills were proposed in 1978, none the following year, and one in 1980. By 1981 there was almost no congressional interest in regulating rDNA research.[7] Any remaining interest focused not on the physical risks but on the ethical and legal ramifications of the research and on the genetically-engineered products that would eventually be commercially marketed.

At the local political level, the flurry of regulations that seemed so imminent in 1977 also failed to materialize. The few laws that were imposed essentially required conformance to the NIH guidelines. No funds were appropriated and no local governmental agencies were created to regulate rDNA research. Meanwhile, the NIH revised its guidelines in 1978, 1980, 1981, and 1982, each time making more rDNA experiments permissible at ever lower levels of containment.

Why Did Concern Evaporate?

Why is the case of regulating rDNA research so dramatically different from that of nuclear power? One possibility is that there has been a growing conservative, antigovernment, antiregulation mood in the nation since the early 1980s. However, this reason does not explain the continuing public concern over nuclear power, acid rain, and other technology-related issues. Another possible explanation is that the risks of recombinant DNA research are lower than those of nuclear power. This assumption runs counter to the opinions of esteemed scientists who have been arguing for years that the risks of nuclear power are far lower than other widely accepted activities such as burning coal for fuel, flying in airplanes, and driving automobiles. However, the public has not accepted this testimony from scientists. Why, in the case of rDNA research, should scientists' views have been accepted?

Perhaps the most striking difference between the two cases is that the scientific community reached more of a consensus about the risks of rDNA research than they did about the risks of nuclear power. Continuing disputes among the experts seem to lead to ongoing conflicts about policy. In all the cases cited in this book, scientists triggered the initial concern and then played prominent roles in the subsequent debates. Members of Congress, interest groups, and the media inevitably joined in, but because of the technical nature of the issues, they relied on the opinions of the experts. This pattern emerges repeatedly. On issues ranging from the arms race to carcinogens in the workplace to the prospects of future energy technologies, Senator X cites the testimony of an esteemed scientist from a prestigious scientific body, only to be countered by Senator Y, who cites opposite testimony by an equally esteemed scientist from an equally prestigious university.[8]

For nuclear power, the most vivid example of such conflict among experts was the dispute over the Rasmussen report. This major study of reactor safety, sponsored in 1975 by the Atomic Energy Commission and directed by MIT Professor Norman Rasmussen, estimated that the worst plausible reactor accident would lead to thirty-three hundred early fatalities, forty-five thousand early illnesses, and fifteen hundred latent cancer fatalities. However, it gave the probability of such a severe accident as one in a billion (per reactor per year).

Nuclear power advocates seized on this report as support for their cause. The exceedingly low probability of an accident, they argued, demonstrated the safety of nuclear power. But others, including the American Physical Society, countered that because of substantial uncertainties (such as those discussed in chapter 3), the likelihood and effects of a serious accident could be considerably greater than estimated. The effects of low-level radiation alone would add several thousand to the estimated latent cancer fatalities.[9]

By 1985 the debate over the Rasmussen report still had not been resolved. Studies by the American Nuclear Society and the nuclear industry, motivated in part by the Three Mile Island accident, indicated that the report had overestimated by as much as a thousand times the amount of radioactive fission products actually released in an accident. If agreement could be reached on the validity of the new figures, a significant easing of restrictions on nuclear power might be justified. But the report's optimistic findings were at least partially contradicted by an American Physical Society study group that found that in some types of accidents the release might be greater than had been estimated.[10]

Initially, the rDNA research debate also was characterized by disagreements within the scientific community. It was a group of scientists who first raised the alarm about rDNA research and who insisted, despite the skepticism of some of their colleagues, on assessing the risks. But once the NIH guidelines were established, the politics of the rDNA debate began to change. By 1977 the scientific community seemed to have closed ranks on the issue, and it presented to Congress and the media a far more united front on the risks of rDNA research than it ever had on the risks of any other major technological policy issue. In one forum after another, one prestigious spokesperson after another—including some who had initially urged caution—argued that the earlier concerns had been greatly overstated.[11]

To be sure, skeptics were still to be found, but many were associated with public interest groups rather than mainstream scientific organizations and were vastly outweighed in prestige and number by proponents of rDNA research. There was no equivalent in the rDNA debate to the dissenting opinion posed by the American Physical Society to the Rasmussen report's estimates of reactor safety. Instead, the majority of scientists

favored expanded rDNA research, and, faced with this pre-
dominant opinion, most of those advocating extensive regulation backed down. Senator Kennedy withdrew support from
his own bill to regulate rDNA research, which had been the
leading piece of such legislation in the Senate.

It is clear that a consensus in the scientific community on
rDNA research and a lack of consensus about nuclear power
at least partly accounts for the differences in policy directions
between the two technologies. But why were scientists able to
come to near consensus about rDNA research and not about
nuclear power? We return again to our original question: what
is it about the rDNA research controversy that has made it so
different from our other cases?

Several critics have suggested that the scientific community
closed ranks because it had a vested interest in ending the
regulatory debate. Unlike nuclear power, where regulations
restrict industry, regulations of rDNA research would have
restricted scientific endeavors. Regulations would have constrained both researchers working in universities and the growing number of scientists who were finding lucrative opportunities in the nascent rDNA industry. As long as they did not fear
outside control, the critics contended, scientists expressed
their doubts freely; once the threat of regulation beyond their
control developed, scientists quickly closed ranks and covered
over their differences about the risks.[12]

Similarly, it can also be argued that because the NIH was
both funding rDNA research and regulating it, this may have
created a bias that led scientists to understate the risks. Scientists seeking research grants obviously had an incentive to
avoid antagonizing the NIH, their potential sponsor. In 1978
Joseph Califano, the secretary of the Department of Health,
Education, and Welfare, ruled that representatives of public
interest groups should be added to the Recombinant Advisory
Committee, but by that point the controversy was already
waning. On the other hand, scientists can advance their ca-
reers by challenging mainstream views with solid research, so
there are also incentives to speak out as well as acquiesce.
And in the case of nuclear power, the Atomic Energy Commission was in the same position as the NIH—funding as well

as regulating nuclear research and development—and still vigorous disputes about nuclear power risks occurred. While it would be surprising if self-interest did not have some role in the resolution of the rDNA research issue, it is not a sufficient explanation, and we must explore further to understand the rDNA research story.

Containing Hazards and Verifying Risks

The most distinctive characteristic of rDNA research is that the risks proved relatively manageable. The consequences of potential accidents could be limited, and estimates of risk could be verified. Therefore, the inherent nature of the problem was different from that posed by nuclear power or by most other risky technologies, and a consensus about the risks was much easier to achieve.

Strategies to limit hazards

While it is impossible to be absolutely certain that the consequences of a serious rDNA research accident will be contained, the probability of containing such accidents within acceptable limits is substantially higher than for nuclear reactor accidents. In addition to requiring that steps be taken to prevent accidents, the NIH relied on two tactics for limiting such hazards.[13] First, and reminiscent of the early approach to reactor safety, the NIH required both physical and biological containment. The NIH classified all permissible rDNA experiments according to their level of potential hazard. The greater the potential hazard, the more extensive the containment requirements. For example, according to the original NIH guidelines, experiments in the high potential hazard class could only be performed in labs of monolithic construction that were equipped with air locks, systems for decontaminating air, autoclaves, shower rooms, and other physical containment safeguards.

Biological containment also was required for more dangerous experiments.[14] Scientists were required to use as host organisms only bacteria that had been shown in animal and human tests to be so enfeebled that they could not survive outside the lab. In this way, even should an accident occur during a hazardous experiment and physical containment fail, biological containment (the inability of the organism to survive outside the lab) would limit the hazard. Even experiments in the least hazardous category had to use only approved bacteria as the host organism. The most common host organism was *E. coli* K-12, a laboratory strain of a common, well-studied colon bacterium (*Escherichia coli*).

The NIH also limited potential hazards by prohibiting particularly risky experiments. Originally, six classes of experiments were banned: (1) experiments with more than ten liters of culture; (2) experiments in which organisms containing rDNA were deliberately released into the environment (such as the one delayed by Judge Sirica in 1984); (3) experiments using DNA from certain pathogens; (4) experiments using DNA segments that code for vertebrate toxins; (5) experiments using rDNA techniques to create certain plant pathogens; and (6) experiments in which drug resistance traits were transferred to disease-causing organisms. These prohibitions were not absolute, since the NIH would make exceptions if sufficient safety precautions were demonstrated.

Prohibiting risky experiments was a very simple method of limiting hazards. To apply this method to nuclear power, reactors would either have to be limited to sizes that would virtually guarantee containment or be prohibited from any place except very remote areas.

Being able to limit the consequences of an accident from rDNA research simplified the NIH's task. The alternative would have been to rely primarily on prevention, which, as we have seen for nuclear reactors, is a difficult strategy to implement in practice. Limiting harm from accidents is simpler than trying to prevent accidents altogether. Regulators were thus able to focus on the relatively limited problem of estimating and protecting against the worst potential consequences of accidents. This is by no means a trivial task, but it is more manageable than trying to anticipate all possible causes of accidents.

Ways to Verify Risks

For both nuclear reactors and rDNA research, reputable experts argued that the risks were acceptably low, but such claims were much more easily verified for rDNA research than they were for nuclear power. Substantial efforts have been made to assess the risks of rDNA research. At least sixteen categories of risks have been identified as shown below:[15]

Gordon Conference, 1973. Risks: new types of plasmids and viruses; large-scale preparation of animal viruses.

Asilomar Conference, February 1975. Risks: spread of antibiotic-resistant organisms; alteration of the host range of bacteria; and "shotgun" experiments with unknown outcomes.

Senate Health Subcommittee, April 1975. Risks: infections not susceptible to known therapies; animal tumor virus genes in bacteria.

Director's Advisory Committee Meeting, February 1976. Risks: new routes of infection; novel pathogens; disease transmitted by *E. coli.*

Senate Health Subcommittee, 1976. Risks: spread of "experimental cancer"; virulent hybrids due to combining two mild viruses; unknown impact on biosphere if new species created.

House Science and Technology Subcommittee, 1977. Risks: altering the course of evolution; transmission of laboratory recombinants to wild strains of bacteria; colonizability of *E. coli.*

National Academy of Sciences Forum, 1977. Risks: latent tumor viruses; insulin genes in *E. coli;* extraintestinal *E. coli* infections; breakdown products of recombinant DNA molecules.

Senate Health Subcommittee, 1977. Risks: possible interference with human autoimmune system; unanticipated hazards; disturbance of metabolic pathways.

Falmouth Workshop, 1977. Risks: creation of more dangerous bacteria; spread of R-factors.

Ascot Workshop, 1978. Risks: penetration into intestinal lining; new types of experiments with viruses.

Workshop on Agricultural Pathogens, 1978. Risks: *E. coli* transformed into a plant pathogen; more virulent strains of plant pathogens.

These hazards have been discussed at more than a dozen scientific workshops and conferences, analyzed through experiments, and reviewed by the Recombinant Advisory Committee, the NIH, the Office of Technology Assessment, and other federal organizations. Much of the research has attempted to answer one or more of the following questions:

Could an organism escape from a laboratory and establish itself in humans, animals, or other parts of the natural environment?

Could a recombinant organism transfer its rDNA to other organisms?

Could the rDNA make the escaped organism dangerous to man or the environment?

From the outset, some scientists asserted that the answer to all of these questions is "no." But the majority of scientists originally said, in effect, "We do not know, so we will have to proceed cautiously until we find out." Their attempts to answer these key questions are an important part of the rDNA story and reveal a great deal about the task of averting catastrophe.

Survival of organisms outside the lab.   The most likely way that organisms could escape from a research laboratory, many scientists believed, was by their unwitting ingestion by a lab worker. At least four sets of studies were performed in which large amounts of *E. coli* K-12 (up to ten billion organisms) were fed to volunteers. All of the organisms died in a few days, and none were passed out in the stool of the volunteers. In another study, fecal cultures from sixty-four lab personnel working with *E. coli* K-12 were periodically obtained over two years. The workers used no precautions other than standard microbiological techniques. At no time in the two years was *E. coli* K-12 recovered in the stool, and this again suggested inability of the bacteria to survive outside the lab.[16] These findings, among others, were interpreted as follows in a letter to the NIH from the chairman of a conference of infectious disease experts held at Falmouth, Massachusetts, in June 1977: "On the basis of extensive tests already completed, it appears that *E. coli* K-12 does not implant in the intestinal tract of man."[17]

There were some qualifications to this conclusion, however, as was attested to in the chairman's summary of the published professional proceedings of the Falmouth conference:

> A number of variables are known to influence the colonization of organisms in the intestinal tract. Implantation can be altered by antibiotic administration, starvation, the type of diet, reduction in gastric acid, and antimotility drugs. It is clear that more implantation experiments need to be performed with attention to these variables, many of which may be found in laboratory workers exposed to these organisms.[18]

The report acknowledged that certain strains of *E. coli* can implant under certain conditions. Persons undergoing antibiotic treatment, for example, are susceptible.[19] The NIH subsequently established laboratory practice guidelines to protect against some such dangers, but it is questionable whether the guidelines are enforceable. Overall, however, a great majority of scientists working in this field concluded that the probability of hazard was too low to take precautions beyond those that are standard in microbiological work.

Transmission to other organisms. Even if some of the organisms escaped, they would soon die unless they could establish themselves in a human, animal, or other part of the natural environment. Research has also been conducted to evaluate this possibility. In more than thirty years of use in genetics laboratories, *E. coli* K-12 has a perfect safety record, and in a study of almost four thousand laboratory-acquired infections, only two involved any type of *E. coli*. In neither of these cases was the infection passed on to another person.[20] Moreover, large numbers of organisms would have to be ingested in order for a human to develop an intestinal illness. This requires more than personal contact—usually a grossly contaminated source of food or water. Given contemporary sanitation and food standards, it was judged highly improbable that an infected laboratory worker could start an epidemic of gastrointestinal illness.

Again, however, this conclusion must be qualified. *E. coli* can cause diseases outside the intestine, and in these cases it takes fewer organisms to produce such illnesses. But most of the rDNA research scientists concluded that transmission of genetically altered organisms would be very unlikely.[21]

Creating a dangerous organism. Even if escape and transmission of organisms containing recombined genes is very unlikely, it is not impossible. If a dangerous organism were created and somehow did escape, the consequences conceivably could be catastrophic. Therefore, research was conducted to examine the likelihood that a dangerous organism might unwittingly be created. In one class of rDNA experiments, known as "shot-gun" experiments, the genes of a plant or animal cell were cut into many segments, and these were inserted at the same time randomly into *E. coli* K-12. These experiments in particular raised fears of an unwitting creation of harmful organisms. To test these fears, the Recombinant Advisory Committee recommended a so-called worst-case experiment that the NIH agreed to fund.

The intention of the worst-case experiment was to see if a dangerous organism could be created deliberately. Investigators inserted the DNA for a virus into *E. coli,* and then administered the altered organisms to mice. Only one of thirteen experimental combinations produced illness and at a rate much lower than the virus would have caused without the DNA manipulation. Most scientists found the experiment reassuring; as one biochemist put it: "This type of experiment is therefore safer than handling the virus itself . . . and a major lowering of the required containment levels seems clearly justified."[22] Again, however, this conclusion required qualification. According to several critics, the one case of viral infection was a new disease pathway not possible without the rDNA techniques.[23]

In another series of experiments to evaluate risks, scientists inserted a similarly altered organism in hamsters to test tumor formation. No tumors developed under normal experimental conditions, but under less likely experimental conditions, where two copies of the virus were inserted simultaneously (as might accidentally occur) tumors were produced. The researchers interpreted this evidence as supporting the safety of the research, as did most other scientists. However, a small minority again dissented and criticized the experimenters' methodology and interpretations.[24]

Because of studies such as these, rDNA research seemed less threatening, and subsequent research reinforced this impression. The gene structure of plants and animals was shown to be significantly different from the gene structure of bacteria. Plant or animal DNA must be altered deliberately to make it compatible with the host if it is to become an active part of the bacteria into which the genes are inserted.[25] Similarly, in most rDNA experiments, the new segment of genes constitutes no more than 0.5 to 1 percent of the total gene set of the host organism. Unless this segment is carefully and deliberately integrated with the host's genes, the host is unlikely to be significantly affected.[26]

Another worst-case scenario was that *E. coli* bacteria containing rDNA designed to produce insulin were assumed to have escaped from the lab, established themselves in the human intestine (and replaced all the normal intestinal *E. coli*), and produced the maximum amount of insulin. Even given these assumptions, the analysts concluded that the total amount of insulin that could be produced would "not be expected to have much, if any effect, on a mammalian host." The results of the analysis, when generalized to more active proteins, indicated that most experiments would pose little problem.[27]

The risk that rDNA can turn a host into a pathogen was

summarized at another important meeting held in 1978 at Ascot, England, and attended by twenty-seven scientists, most of whom were virologists:

> The workshop concluded that inserting part or all of the gene set of viruses into *E. coli* K-12, with approved vectors, poses "no more risk than work with the infectious virus or its nucleic acid and in most, if not all cases, clearly presents less risk. In fact, . . . cloning of viral DNA in *E. coli* K-12 may produce a unique opportunity to study with greatly reduced risks the biology of extremely pathogenic and virulent viruses." In other words, inserting a piece of viral DNA into *E. coli* K-12 locks it up inside the bacterium and makes it much safer to handle than the naked virus itself.[28]

A few scientists did not share this view, but the great majority believed that the evidence showed it to be very unlikely that genetically altered bacteria would be dangerous in the unlikely event that they did escape and the even more unlikely event that they established themselves in the environment.

Appraisal of risks

These experiments and analyses do not show that there is no risk from rDNA research, and in fact they reveal that risks can arise in certain, very specific, highly unlikely conditions. But such controlled experimentation and the data generated through experience led a great majority of scientists and experts to conclude that most of the early concerns about rDNA research were unfounded. The ability to practically assess risk is the essential difference between the nuclear power and rDNA research issues. Much of the analysis of reactor safety is hypothetical, focusing on unlikely conditions that might arise during events that have never occurred. In developing policy about rDNA research, by contrast, policy makers have been able to make such analyses on a more concrete basis; risks have been evaluated by empirical tests governed by usual scientific methods and standards.

The concrete nature of this evaluation has had an enormous effect on the regulatory process. As confidence grew that *E.*

coli K-12 was unlikely to survive outside the lab or be dangerous if it did, the guidelines governing rDNA research were
gradually relaxed. In 1978 the requirements for biological containment in experiments using *E. coli* K-12 were reduced to
the lowest level, and in 1981 most classes of experiments using
E. coli K-12 were exempted from the guidelines altogether.
Moreover, new host systems were approved for use, the NIH
abolished or reduced restrictions on most experiments not using *E. coli* K-12, and by spring 1982 there was no longer a
category of prohibited experiments.

Conclusions

In chapter 7 we will describe the major characteristics
of a catastrophe-aversion system that is at least partially illustrated in each of our cases. The history of recombinant DNA
research provides the clearest example of such a system in
operation. When concerns about the risks of rDNA emerged,
steps were taken to protect against potential catastrophe. Certain classes of experiments were altogether banned, and all
others had to be performed within biological and physical containment. Once precautions had been taken, attempts were
made to learn more about the risks, both by deliberate testing
and by monitoring experience. As more was learned about the
risks and as concerns decreased, the initial precautions were
progressively relaxed.

Critics have argued that this strategy should have been implemented more stringently. It is true that testing could have
been more thorough, the burden of proof could have been
kept more squarely on the advocates of potentially risky research for a longer period, nonscientists could have been given
more decision-making authority earlier in the process, more of
the opposing scientific opinions could have been evaluated,
more experiments could have been prohibited, and the guidelines could have been relaxed more slowly.

How cautiously to proceed in protecting against potential
risks is always a matter of judgment as well as a matter of
science. In the case of rDNA research, a substantial majority

of experts in the field agreed that the risks were very low. The NIH, local governments, and members of Congress went along with this judgment, and these judgments have been borne out by experience. Former critics of rDNA research no longer are vocal about the dangers—perhaps persuaded at last or maybe just overwhelmed. Whether or not the critics were correct, sensible strategies were developed to cope with the uncertainties and potential risks of rDNA research. We discuss these strategies in more detail in our concluding chapters.

A secondary point in this chapter has concerned the striking difference in the fates of the public debates over rDNA research and nuclear power. We have argued that this difference can be attributed largely to the differing natures of the two problems. In rDNA, a worst-case event can be contained and estimates of risk can be tested empirically. A worst-case event for a nuclear reactor cannot be contained and therefore must be prevented; and estimates of risk must necessarily remain hypothetical. Although one side or the other in the nuclear controversy may be mistaken, there is a sound reason why no strategy has been developed that can resolve the debate.

If the objective nature of the technological issue affects its fate, what about the many other explanations for technology policy debates? And how does the objective nature of a technology relate to the widely accepted view that public perceptions and fears are what really guide technology debates and shape policy? We believe that the nature of a social problem limits what constitutes legitimate debate. The nature of the problem in the nuclear power debate is such that there is no way to establish definitively the magnitude of the risks. Advocates of nuclear power can insist that the probabilities of accidents are very low, that the major causes of accidents have been anticipated, and that the worst case would not really be that bad, but none of these arguments can be fully verified. Regulators are left with no conclusive basis for deciding between these claims and opposite claims. Lacking a basis for resolving the facts of the matter, factors like public perceptions and general attitudes become important. The position one takes on the conflicting estimates of the risks depends on whether one trusts government institutions, whether one fears high technology, and so on.

In contrast, the nature of the rDNA problem imposed objective constraints on the resulting debate. Once studies demonstrated that *E. coli* K-12 was highly unlikely to survive outside the lab and cause epidemics, the credibility of counterclaims about high risks diminished. The burden then shifted to the opposition to provide evidence, based on experience or experiments, that the risks were in fact as great as claimed. In other words, the facts constrained the debate. Such "facts," determined at any given time by scientific consensus, may later prove to be mistaken; until that time, they restrict the range of legitimate disagreement. And they constrain the currency of the debate as well, since only new "facts" are sufficient to displace old ones.

It is important to note that the discussion in this chapter has been limited to the physical risks of recombinant DNA research. As commercial biotechnology products are introduced, a new set of potential risks and regulatory issues is emerging. Moreover, as scientific techniques become increasingly powerful, debates surely will arise over the propriety of intervention into the human gene structure.[29] Whether appropriate strategies will be developed for handling these ethical and philosophical issues remains to be seen. To the extent feasible, the strategies used in the rDNA research controversy will be worth emulating.

5

Threats to the Ozone Layer

Some of the key strategies used in regulating toxic chemicals, nuclear power, and recombinant DNA are less applicable to technologies that pose atmospheric threats. The potential catastrophe cannot be contained, as it can to a considerable extent in a nuclear reactor or in a biological research laboratory. Once problems occur in the atmosphere, the consequences cannot readily be reversed or mitigated as is possible with some pesticides and other toxic substances. Yet changes in the earth's atmosphere are even more potentially threatening than chemical or nuclear disasters. To put it callously, humanity could do without Buffalo (Love Canal) or Harrisburg (Three Mile Island) much more easily than it could live without a benign global atmosphere.

The following two chapters examine whether we have a system for coping with such atmospheric threats. Chapter 6 deals with the greenhouse effect—the climatic changes that may result from increasing emissions of carbon dioxide and other gases. Serious problems appear to be perhaps half a century in the future, so the greenhouse case can provide insight into how society heeds early warnings and plans advance action. In contrast, this chapter focuses on an atmospheric threat on which some action has already occurred: possible depletion of the ozone layer that protects humans and other species from excessive ultraviolet radiation.

Ozone is formed and destroyed by a large number of photochemical processes in the upper atmosphere. For example, ultraviolet radiation from the sun catalyzes the combination of atmospheric oxygen molecules with free oxygen atoms to form ozone. The strongest concentrations of ozone occur in the upper stratosphere, some twenty miles above the earth's surface.[1] This ozone layer absorbs ultraviolet radiation and thereby substantially cuts down the amount that reaches the earth's surface.

Initial Concerns: The SST

It was not until about 1970 that scientists began to realize that human activities could damage the ozone layer and thereby alter climate and harm terrestrial life. The first warning came in a Boeing Company scientist's internal report that was not intended for public release. It suggested that exhaust gases from the supersonic transport (SST) would induce a number of environmental changes, including an increase in water vapor in the stratosphere that could lead to partial depletion of the ozone layer.

This report was a result of Boeing's efforts "to answer the opposition of conservation groups and the concerns of numerous independent scientists" about the SST.[2] It had the effect of spurring opposition, however, when the estimates were obtained and used by Representative Henry S. Reuss (Democrat, Wisconsin), who was trying to mobilize Congress to withhold funding from the SST project. The report's author, Dr. Halstead Harrison, later disavowed his original conclusions, saying that they were early "back-of-envelope stuff" that had been disconfirmed by more sophisticated analysis. According to Harrison, the early research was part of a "devil's advocate exercise," and the calculations had been based on worst-case assumptions about how the atmosphere works. Revised estimates showed that a full fleet of SSTs might reduce ozone by "only 3.8 percent."[3]

Meanwhile, the Study of Critical Environmental Problems (SCEP), sponsored by the Massachusetts Institute of Technology, was examining the possibility that exhaust emissions from an SST fleet could cause smog in the stratosphere in the same way that automobile emissions cause smog at ground level. SCEP found that particles released into the stratosphere could affect global climate and were therefore a source of "genuine concern"; but "reduction of ozone due to interaction with water vapor or other exhaust gases should be insignificant."[4] Unknown to SCEP, however, other atmospheric scientists doing basic research unrelated to the SST issue were rapidly improving their understanding of the chemical reactions that affect ozone in the atmosphere; their findings suggested that water vapor was not the critical factor in the ozone balance.

Stimulated partly by this emerging information and partly by a federally sponsored conference on SST environmental problems, atmospheric chemist Harold S. Johnston performed calculations in early 1971 that suggested nitrogen oxides from SST exhausts would pose a much greater threat to the ozone layer than would water vapor. A full fleet of five hundred SSTs operating for seven hours per day could destroy up to half of the earth's ozone layer, not the small percentage that other scientists had estimated based on the belief that water vapor was the threat. *The New York Times* reported that Johnston had predicted that such a change would occur in less than a year after a full SST fleet began operations, but Johnston made a far more cautious appraisal in his article in *Science*.[5]

Numerous other factors affected the 1971 congressional decision not to approve construction of a supersonic transport jet. Key concerns were the effects of sonic booms in populated areas and the high cost of the project, but the ozone threat was also a significant drawback.

The Effects of Fluorocarbons

A second threat to the ozone layer was suggested in late 1973 by University of California chemists Mario J. Molina and F. Sherwood Rowland. They proposed that fluorocarbons from aerosol propellants, refrigerators, and air conditioners could pose a severe threat to the ozone layer.[6] Such ozone damage, in turn, "might cause awesome changes in the earth's weather and ecology, including damage to wildlife and crops."[7] Each percentage decrease in ozone, the scientists theorized, would result in a 2 percent increase in skin cancer. Published in June 1974 in *Nature*, this theory received immediate attention from the scientific community, the media, and government.[8]

Fluorocarbons, also called halogenated chlorofluoromethanes (CFMs), chlorofluorocarbons (CFCs), or halocarbons, are organic chemical compounds not found in nature. They are synthesized from carbon, chlorine, and fluorine. Chemically inert, they do not react with most substances. This means that they are not toxic, and are excellent for aerosols because they will not contaminate the product. Because they are nonflammable, fluorocarbons are much safer in refrigerators and air conditioners than are the available substitutes, such as ammonia, methyl chloride, and sulfur dioxide. Fluorocarbons have been used as refrigerants since the 1930s and in aerosols since the Second World War.

The potential threat posed by fluorocarbons is that they are complex molecules that can be broken down into their constituent atoms under certain conditions. The Molina-Rowland theory specified five steps to the process:

1. Fluorocarbons are carried by winds to the stratosphere; this process can take as long as ten years.

2. Once in the stratosphere, the fluorocarbon compound is broken down by ultraviolet light into its constituent chemicals, including the element chlorine.

3. The released chlorine reacts chemically with ozone to convert it to atmospheric oxygen, which is less effective than ozone in absorbing ultraviolet radiation.[9]

4. Subsequent chemical reactions allow a single chlorine molecule to continue to interact with tens of thousands of ozone molecules; thus, there is a substantial multiplier effect.

5. Ozone depletion allows more ultraviolet radiation to reach the earth's surface, resulting in an increase in skin

cancer among susceptible individuals and perhaps harming crops and animals. Ozone depletion also may alter the temperature of the stratosphere and thereby alter global weather patterns.

Confirmation of the fluorocarbon theory and risks

As in the case of recombinant DNA (and as distinguished from the case of nuclear power), a majority of scientists quickly became convinced of the accuracy of the Molina-Rowland theory of ozone depletion. How did such agreement come about?

As with rDNA, the ability to test for risks appears to have been the key factor in this agreement. Fellow researchers quickly tested various components of the theory. By late 1975 the physicist Arthur L. Schmeltekopf of the National Oceanic and Atmospheric Administration reported that "fluorocarbons are getting to the stratosphere in the predicted amounts."[10] This finding was based on air samples collected by weather balloons at heights of up to 17.4 miles (midstratosphere).

The same experiment also helped confirm that fluorocarbon compounds were being broken down in the stratosphere. Above a level of about 9.3 miles, the amount of fluorocarbons in the air samples began to diminish, and only traces remained at the highest levels sampled. So it was clear that "something is destroying the fluorocarbons . . . at the rates predicted by theory."[11]

Other independent experiments, conducted under laboratory conditions rather than in the stratosphere, found that fluorocarbon molecules split when bombarded by light from ultraviolet lamps. Depending on conditions, either one or two chlorine atoms were released from each fluorocarbon molecule. From these experiments, National Bureau of Standards chemist Peter J. Ausloos concluded that "we have proved beyond any doubt that you get chlorine atoms when a photon [of light] is absorbed by the fluorocarbon molecule."[12]

So the first steps in the Molina-Rowland theory had been quickly confirmed; even the affected industries conceded this point within about a year. But would fluorocarbons break down ozone under the actual conditions prevailing in the atmosphere? Direct measurements of ozone levels had been made for other purposes since the late 1950s, and steps were taken to expand and supplement these measurements. Interpretation of the results was difficult, however, because ozone levels fluctuate daily by as much as 25 percent, vary with the season, and differ markedly over various parts of the globe. As a result, most scientists doubted that direct measurements could be used to confirm the Molina-Rowland theory until about 5 percent ozone depletion had occurred. Only then would any depletion caused by human activity be dramatic enough to distinguish it from natural variances.

Scientists resorted, therefore, to less direct methods of testing the hypothesized chlorine-ozone reaction. If such a reaction were occurring, there would be other changes in the chemistry of the stratosphere, and some of these changes might be easier to measure than ozone. For example, some of the chlorine released from fluorocarbons would be expected to form hydrochloric acid (HCl). Scientists at the Jet Propulsion Laboratory (at California Institute of Technology) designed experiments using U-2 flights and weather balloons to measure HCl levels in the stratosphere. Finding higher HCl concentrations in the upper atmosphere than at lower levels, they concluded: "The results show very clearly that there is a stratospheric source of hydrochloric acid—that it doesn't get there in that form from the earth."[13]

A variety of other experiments likewise contributed to the validation of the Molina-Rowland hypothesis.[14]

At this point political judgment had to be exercised. Granted that fluorocarbons would have some effect on atmospheric ozone, was the effect significant enough to regulate? Various interest groups, scientists, and governments had substantially different answers to this policy question.

Industry argued that the ozone-depletion theory should be proven before the government took regulatory action. Some $400 to $450 million per year in fluorocarbon product sales were at stake in the United States alone. In the words of an industry spokesperson, there was "enough doubt to warrant making a better test in nature before demolishing a major industry."[15] As expressed in one 1975 industry paper: "The questions aren't just whether the theory's general premises are valid, but also whether the magnitude of any ultimate effect is meaningful to the quality of the environment and public health."[16]

The American Chemical Society complained during the height of the dispute that any restriction on fluorocarbons would constitute "the first regulation to be based entirely on an unverified scientific prediction." Such an action, the professional group declared, would set "a very dangerous precedent."[17] Likewise, a DuPont spokesperson protested proposed regulations, arguing that "what's happening is disturbing and alarming. We're going a very long way into the regulatory process before the scientists know what's really going on."[18]

Government advisory bodies, in contrast, recommended quick action to prevent potential dangers. In 1975, just one year after the original publication of the Molina-Rowland theory, a federal task force reported that fluorocarbons constituted "a legitimate cause for concern." Unless new evidence contradicted the data then available, the task force concluded that fluorocarbons should be banned for newly manufactured refrigerators and air conditioners. It was taken for granted that fluorocarbon aerosols should be banned.[19] As a result, the Environmental Protection Agency conducted an economic impact assessment of possible regulations for limiting the fluorocarbon threat.[20]

A panel of the National Research Council (NRC) was convened in 1975 to again review the evidence of fluorocarbon dangers. Reporting in spring 1976, the panel scaled down the depletion estimate but confirmed the existence of a potentially severe danger.[21] Additional federal studies followed in rapid succession and averaged at least one per year through 1984.[22] While the United States led the way, research was intensified in almost every industrial nation, typically under governmental sponsorship.[23]

Governmental restrictions on fluorocarbons

The Molina-Rowland ozone theory had reached the major newspapers by fall 1974, and it was the subject of a congressional hearing that December.[24] In 1975 additional hearings were held before the House Commerce Committee, the House Science and Technology Committee, and at least one committee in the Senate. As a result, the House Commerce Committee added an ozone provision to the Clean Air Act amendments of 1977.

This legislation called for research and periodic assessment of the ozone-fluorocarbon problem and gave EPA until late 1978 to issue regulations restricting or banning the use of fluorocarbons in aerosol sprays if the agency concluded that the chemicals could "reasonably be anticipated to cause or contribute to the endangerment of public health or welfare." (The legislation authorized EPA to issue regulations even earlier if the agency found a "significant risk" from the sprays.) Although EPA waited for an NRC report, which recommended that action be delayed pending further study, EPA went ahead and banned most aerosol uses of fluorocarbons in 1978. There were a few exemptions for high priority needs where available substitutes were considered unsatisfactory (for instance, for some pharmaceuticals in spray form). U.S. manufacturers had begun to phase out aerosols well before the legislation and subsequent ban took effect.

The 1977 Clean Air Act also authorized EPA to propose restrictions on nonaerosol sources of fluorocarbons. The agency considered banning the use of fluorocarbon refrigerants but retreated from the idea, partly in response to manufacturers' arguments that economic substitutes were not available. Instead, EPA in 1980 proposed a rule to limit increases in overall U.S. production of fluorocarbons (there are further details later in this chapter). These proposed production limits resulted in some two thousand formal complaints, with much of the opposition coming from a coalition of about five hundred corporations called "The Alliance for Responsible CFC Policy." Nevertheless, EPA announced in March 1982 that regulations would soon be proposed that would limit fluorocarbon production to 1981 levels, but no proposal was ever actually made.

By 1980 only Sweden and Canada had joined the United States in banning fluorocarbon aerosols. Denmark and Norway soon followed suit, but a majority of European nations did not. The European Economic Community subsequently cut back on aerosols to some extent and has halted construction of additional fluorocarbon manufacturing capacity.[25] Since existing capacity is expected to be underutilized until the turn of the century, this step has had no real effect on emission levels. The United States, Canada, and a handful of other nations have continued trying to persuade the majority of nations to adopt tougher controls on fluorocarbons. In 1985 forty-three nations signed an international treaty providing for cooperative research and agreed to meet in 1987 to consider formal international controls. As part of the pact, the Soviet Union for the first time agreed to provide information on its fluorocarbon usage.[26]

Fertilizers and Other Threats

While research on fluorocarbons was proceeding, it became apparent that there could be other sources of damage to the ozone layer. Nitrogenous fertilizers were identified as a threat in 1974; like the SST, they too contribute nitrogen oxides to the atmosphere. Most nitrogen oxide is produced in the oceans and is thus not within human control; human-induced changes in soil acidity (for instance, from acid rain) and use of nitrogen fertilizers are the principal ways humans add to the natural rates of nitrogen oxide production.[27] In 1976 the first quantitative estimate of possible ozone depletion from fertilizer was calculated at approximately 10 percent.[28] Other scholars pointed to the partially offsetting effects of other atmospheric and soil chemistry processes that could be expected to reduce the extent of the problem from fertilizers.[29]

By 1977 increases in worldwide fertilizer use led one scientist to argue that this source could constitute the principal long-term threat to the ozone layer (see Figure 2).[30] A 1978 NRC report partially endorsed this view.[31] Subsequent NRC ozone studies have given about equal attention to nitrogen oxides and fluorocarbons and have also begun to explore other trace gases that pose depletion threats.

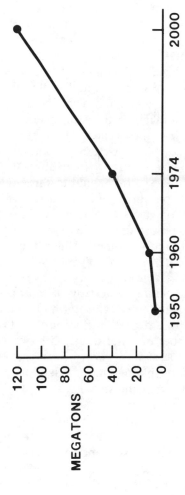

Figure 2.   *World fertilizer use in megatons*

Source: "Will Fertilizers Harm Ozone as Much as SSTs?," *Science* 195 (1977): 658.

Shortly after the SST controversy, an environmental scientist reported that methane produced indirectly by human activities could pose a threat to the ozone layer.[32] Like nitrogen, methane reacts chemically with individual oxygen atoms and reduces the number of free oxygen atoms available to form ozone. Methane is produced primarily by decaying vegetable matter and by intestinal food digestion. Major sources include paddy fields fertilized with human and animal wastes, swamps, and the flatulence of domesticated cattle. While it seems almost a joke, this latter source contributed an estimated 150 million tons of methane to the atmosphere in 1981, a 75 percent increase in just one decade. Termites recently have been shown to produce levels of methane that could be significant when added to other sources. Incredibly, there are approximately 100 million termites (equal to three-quarters of a ton) for every human on earth, and the combined effect of their methane production rivals that of cattle.[33]

A 1979 NRC report drew attention to another potentially significant threat to ozone—methylchloroform. It is used widely as an industrial degreasing solvent, and production of the chemical has been doubling every five years. Less inert than fluorocarbons (so more is destroyed before it can reach the upper atmosphere), methylchloroform nevertheless could lead to substantial ozone depletion if its use continues to increase rapidly.[34] A number of other trace gases—of which carbon tetrachloride is the best known—also carry ozone-depleting chlorine into the stratosphere, and production of most of these chlorocarbons is increasing steadily.[35]

Another chemical that is gaining attention is bromine. Methylbromide now is the largest source of the chemical and its production increased more than 400 percent between 1972 and 1984. Organic bromine also comes from ethylenedibromide, an additive in leaded gasoline and a now-restricted fumigant for agricultural produce. Two of the minor fluorocarbons also contain bromine; their use as fire extinguisher chemicals has been increasing, and atmospheric concentrations have gone up by more than 10 percent annually in recent years. Altogether, if organic bromine concentrations grow by another 400 percent, they could lead to destruction of 4 to 5 percent of global ozone in addition to the depletion caused by chlorine compounds such as the major fluorocarbons.[36]

Ozone Depletion: A Declining Threat?

Refined computer models of the ozone balance and new information about the rate of key chemical reactions have been developed almost every year since 1970. Frequent changes in estimates of ozone depletion have been the result.

A 1979 NRC report suggested eventual ozone depletion at about twice the level indicated in 1976. Continued production and use of ozone-depleting chemicals at current rates, the panel said, would eventually lead to destruction of about 16.5 percent of the world's total stratospheric ozone. Growth in fluorocarbon use, to be expected in the absence of international controls, would exacerbate the problem still further. If the projected 7 percent annual increase in fluorocarbon production occurred up to the year 2000, for example, the panel estimated at least a 30 percent reduction in ozone.[37]

After 1979, however, depletion estimates began to decline. In 1982 the NRC reverted to estimates closer to the 1976 report—in the range of 6 to 12 percent. The NRC projected significantly reduced ozone depletion in the lower stratosphere, in part because recent studies had drawn attention for the first time to unexpected sources of ozone production.[38] Aircraft that fly below an altitude of about ten miles, for example, release nitrogen oxides that undergo chemical reactions to form ozone. This recent research also had begun to take into account the greenhouse effect from heating of the earth's lower atmosphere; this is expected to cool down the stratosphere and thereby slow rates of ozone destruction and speed rates of ozone formation.

Research on the stratosphere and its ozone balance had made enormous progress by 1982. Some discrepancies remained between actual measurements of chemicals in the stratosphere and estimates provided by computer simulation models, but these discrepancies had been reduced greatly in the course of a decade. Even technical prose could not dis-

Figure 3.   Changing ozone depletion estimates

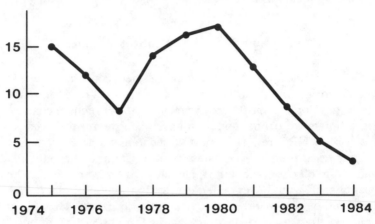

SOURCE: Adapted from National Research Council, *Causes and Effects of Changes in Stratospheric Ozone: Update 1983* (Washington, D.C.: National Academy Press, 1984).

guise many scientists' beliefs that the models were accurately reflecting the true state of the ozone balance. Of one important discrepancy concerning chlorine oxide, for example, the 1982 NRC report said: "Those of us who believe there are grounds to judge the effect [of resolving the discrepancy] . . . conclude that our estimate of ozone reduction from CFC emissions should not change [go up] by more than a factor of two."[39] In other words, they expected that the 1982 prediction would remain relatively stable over time.

But in 1983 new information led to further reduction—down to just 2 to 4 percent—in estimates of ozone depletion. The NRC Committee went so far as to suggest that ozone might even increase by 1 percent![40]

Altogether, as shown in Figure 3, estimates of ozone depletion declined steadily from 1979 to early 1984. There was reason to have greater confidence in these later estimates, since models of the atmosphere now describe some two hundred chemical reactions—over twice the number used in 1974—and the rates of many reactions now are much better known. It began to seem that the ozone controversy was over.

In late 1984 and 1985, however, the picture again changed

for the worse. New research by Harvard scientists indicated that ozone depletion is not linear beyond a certain point.[41] Within two generations, if use of ozone-depleting chemicals continues to increase at the pace set in recent years, concentrations of trace gases in the lower stratosphere could be high enough to trigger an exponential rate of depletion. If so, the scientists calculated, eventual depletion would total approximately 15 percent—almost the same as had been estimated in 1974. A 1985 EPA background paper suggested that even greater ozone destruction is possible, given the sharp increase in fluorocarbon usage that began again in 1983 after nearly a decade of reduced sales.[42] The concept of exponential depletion spurred renewed activity by environmental interest groups, including a federal lawsuit filed by the Natural Resources Defense Council that asked that EPA be required to issue more stringent regulations against ozone-depleting chemicals.[43]

The recent depletion estimates are not as different from those of immediately preceding years as they may seem. The 1983–84 NRC report acknowledges that "total ozone could decrease substantially, perhaps by as much as 10 percent by 2040" under certain circumstances.[44] However, the NRC emphasized a lower figure, as did the media. Why was this? Depletion estimates have always depended on two factors: the rate of depletion induced by a given volume of each chemical, and the amount of each ozone-depleting chemical produced and released into the atmosphere. Only the first factor is scientifically determinable; about the second, scientists have no special expertise, since production levels of chemicals are determined by political and economic factors. Instead of explicitly calling attention to the inevitable uncertainty introduced by this factor, however, most ozone reports have quietly made sensible guesses. Now, for the first time, different groups of scientists are publicly disagreeing about their guesses.

Elements of the Regulatory Strategy

The United States led most of the world in considering the threat to ozone as a danger deserving active response. While there were several serious shortcomings in translating science into public policy, there also were conspicuous strengths. Overall U.S. ozone policy has displayed a very sensible sequence: scientific monitoring revealed a variety of threats; selective actions were taken to limit the potential damage; and further research and debate attempted to reduce remaining uncertainties and thereby clarify the need to implement more stringent regulatory measures.

Detecting the threat

The first strategy, not evident except in retrospect, was deployment of diverse scientists in academic, governmental, and industrial research institutions. These atmospheric chemists and other specialists established a framework within which the ozone problem could begin to be understood. These early researchers were not looking for atmospheric threats but were merely pursuing their own relatively esoteric interests concerning atmosphere and climate. Some were employed by institutions with practical objectives, such as weather forecasting, but most were simply part of the large network of scientists that has developed over the past century. Without anyone planning it, this network has come to constitute an early warning system to alert society about physical threats to the environment and to human health and safety.

This scientific community also provides a means for determining whether the first warnings about a potential threat should be taken seriously. Once Molina and Rowland had offered a speculative theory about the risks of fluorocarbons, their idea was broken down into many smaller, more comprehensible parts; scientists from diverse specialties clarified small parts of the complex theory and reached consensus on its basic accuracy. Thereafter, prestigious National Research Council committees synthesized available scientific knowledge and made this information comprehensible to policy makers. All these are common approaches to complex problems with substantial technical components and are unremarkable except for the fact that many people still do not recognize them as standard operating procedures for monitoring risks.

While it is comforting that scientists have been attempting to clarify the extent of the ozone threat, can we count on scientists to attend to other potential problems from risky technologies? What will draw scientific attention to problems that society needs diagnosed? The case discussed in this chapter indicates at least three incentives.

First, the pioneering efforts of early scientists were stimulated primarily by intellectual curiosity and ordinary career considerations. At a later stage, these motives combined with a desire to help clarify how society should respond to a new threat. (The SST analyses and the series of NRC reports on fluorocarbons are the best examples.) Finally, additional scientists were drawn in when increased funding became available after government was pressed to action by interest groups and concerned government officials. Much of the research on atmospheric threats since about 1975 probably falls in this category. The key point is that all of these routes for focusing scientific attention are predictable ones that we see repeated in many different policy areas. They are part of society's implicit strategy for averting catastrophes.

Protecting against the threat

Once scientists had narrowed the range of credible dispute, the U.S. government acted very rapidly in the SST and fluorocarbon aerosol cases. Other nations moved more slowly, if at all, against these threats, and no nation so far has taken action against the other ozone depleters.

No one knew for sure in the mid-1970s whether there would be any ozone destruction since direct evidence would not be available until several percent depletion had occurred. But *if* depletion were occurring, it could have very severe results. Faced with this possibility, the least risky approach would have been to ban all ozone-depleting chemicals, but this policy would have been extremely costly, if not impossible, to implement. Hence, EPA pursued a more expedient approach: it banned most aerosol sprays while permitting the continued use of fluorocarbons for refrigeration and other purposes considered more essential. Thus, if fluorocarbons turned out to be a problem, at least some reduction in the magnitude of the consequences would have been achieved at an acceptable cost.

Monitoring and debate

The ban on aerosols can be seen as a way of buying time for additional research; it slowed down any ozone destruction caused by U.S. fluorocarbon usage and thereby gained time to determine the magnitude of the threat. In effect, the strategy was to first take readily achievable steps to at least partially protect against the potential hazard and then attempt to reduce uncertainty about the threat before taking more stringent precautions.

This two-step approach also provided time for political innovation and debate. In its 1980 proposal for regulating non-aerosol fluorocarbons, EPA borrowed and extended a distinctive new tactic from Europe: a ceiling on overall production levels and an auction among competing manufacturers to bid for rights to produce fixed quantities of fluorocarbons.[45] As simple as this seems, the idea of quantitative limits on dangerous activities is still relatively novel. The usual approach is to allow activities to occur with unlimited frequency but to restrict the amount of hazard posed by each one; emission controls on automobiles are a typical example.

The second part of the proposal was also innovative. Since manufacturers would have to raise their prices to cover the fees paid to EPA, consumer demand for fluorocarbons probably would drop somewhat. But if demand still exceeded supply, prices would go up until some former fluorocarbon users switched to cheaper substitutes. Thus, "the marketplace would determine what kinds of products using fluorocarbons were produced within the overall limit."[46] This idea of using market-like procedures in place of ordinary command-and-control regulations was championed by many economists during the 1970s, and there have been several experiments with pollution taxes and licenses. But in 1980 it was an innovative approach for a major regulatory endeavor, and it still remains far from ordinary. While EPA did not actually use these tactics in the ozone case, they now are part of the repertoire available for dealing with future threats.

Evidence in the early 1980s seemed to suggest that additional restrictions would not be necessary on production and use of ozone-depleting chemicals. Subsequently, however, fluorocarbon production began to increase rapidly, and new scientific evidence suggests that ozone depletion may be exponential rather than linear. Moreover, the foam-blowing industry is becoming a large user of fluorocarbons, and molded seat cushions are hardly as essential as refrigerants. So there is reason to expect renewed debate about the imposition of more stringent controls on fluorocarbons.

Shortcomings of the strategy

While the U.S. ozone strategy followed a sensible overall course, it had several important limitations. First, the handling of the ozone episode may have reinforced an already excessive tendency of policy makers to substitute scientific analysis for judgment and strategy when regulating risky technologies. When the magnitude of the threat is very uncertain, as it was in this case, scientific analysis has a way of dressing up as "fact" conclusions that actually are based on judgment. Each NRC depletion estimate contained implicit judgments about future increases in use of ozone-depleting chemicals. This did not invalidate the scientific components, but it obscured the tasks facing policy makers.

In considering options for dealing with the ozone threat, the key issue is whether or not to limit increased use of certain chemicals. So growth rates and their effects on depletion estimates are the critical variables. If policy makers are not explicitly made aware of what to expect at low, medium and high rates of increase, they cannot readily monitor whether chemical usage is remaining in the range judged to be an acceptable risk. The NRC ozone committees did not hide their judgments about future increases of ozone-depleting chemicals, but neither did they set forth separate scenarios in case actual growth rates proved higher or lower than expected. Moreover, studies of changes in usage rates for the various chemicals have not been as extensive or as sophisticated as contemporary economic analysis permits.

A related shortcoming in the ozone case concerns society's ability or willingness to respond to a threat. Although it seems counterintuitive, concern about ozone depletion went down as the number of actual threats went up. First, the SST and then fluorocarbons were the focus for alarm, and both evoked considerable public concern. But this concern diminished thereafter, well before scientific evidence became more reassuring. This could be a simple attention-cycle phenomenon, in which the media and the public simply got tired of ozone stories. Or perhaps the problem was too complex—"If it is too hard for me to grasp, I don't want to hear about it."

Furthermore, some of the newer sources of ozone threats, such as nitrogenous fertilizers, are more central to contemporary economic activity and have stronger political constituencies than did the SST and aerosol fluorocarbons. Even if the 1985 estimate of 15 percent depletion survives further scrutiny for a number of years, powerful interest groups are likely to oppose regulatory action in the name of waiting for reduced uncertainty. A political paralysis can thereby develop, based in part on a hope that the next scientific report will have discovered new ozone-producing processes that will make ozone depletion less of a threat. Waiting certainly is easier than deciding how to act, given the factual uncertainties and the known economic costs of regulatory strategies.

In some ways, waiting is intelligent: when a broad range of interests would be affected by regulatory action, it often makes good sense to wait for greater certainty about the threat before taking costly curative actions. Unfortunately, it is difficult to draw the line between prudent waiting and short-sighted preservation of interest.

A third problem revealed in the ozone case is the difficulty of taking concerted action against international threats from risky technologies. Even though it would have been relatively easy to do, many nations did not ban fluorocarbon aerosols. If the ozone threat had materialized as expected in the mid-1970s, considerable damage would have been done before all nations had unambiguous evidence of the danger. In spite of a number of global environmental threats in addition to ozone depleters, there still is no institution strong enough to impose a global perspective on international, national, and industry decision makers. The result is a typical example of the so-called tragedy-of-the-commons predicament: any nation that restricts dangerous products penalizes itself economically and does little to impel global action.

Fortunately, U.S. aerosol usage comprised a large percentage of global fluorocarbon production in the 1970s. Hence, unilateral action by the one nation could temporarily reduce whatever threat the entire world faced. But growing use of a wide variety of ozone depleters throughout the world means that no single nation will be able to have much effect in the future, if additional restrictions come to be warranted.

Finally, the ozone case raises in a new way an issue common to every technological risk in this volume: How safe is safe enough? While the United States took sensible initial precautions against fluorocarbons, even greater caution might have been warranted. It requires as much as a century for atmospheric processes to decompose fluorocarbons; so, if conclusive evidence of ozone depletion were obtained this year and all implicated chemicals were banned immediately, ozone depletion would continue for many years because of the chemicals already put into the atmosphere. There would be a long delay, then, before the effects of an error in ozone policy could be corrected. Under such circumstances, it might make sense to proceed very cautiously in order to avoid getting trapped in an ozone-depletion sequence that could not be halted. More precautions would be costly, but so is inadequate caution. We will have more to say about the "How safe" question in chapter 8.

6

The Greenhouse Threat

In the twenty-first century we face the threat of a major change in global climate caused by human activities, especially combustion of carbon-rich fossil fuels. Because atmospheric carbon dioxide (CO_2) and certain other gases prevent heat radiation from escaping back into space—the greenhouse effect—increasing production of these gases is expected to lead to a warmer earth. The questions are: is this situation potentially catastrophic, how soon could a serious problem arise, and what strategies are available for averting the danger?

Like the ozone threat, the global nature of the greenhouse effect makes many of the usual catastrophe-aversion strategies inappropriate; unlike the ozone case, no action has yet been taken to ameliorate this threat. The delay is due in part to the fact that the problem is not imminent. It is also likely that taking action will be quite difficult, since the greenhouse threat arises primarily from an activity that is absolutely central to contemporary life: the combustion of fossil fuels in pursuit of present-day comforts and affluence. It is much harder for most of us to imagine doing without fossil fuels than it was to forego the use of fluorocarbon aerosols or the SST. When viewed from this perspective, the greenhouse threat poses a formidable challenge.

Sources and Effects of the Greenhouse Problem

The combustion of fossil fuels is one of the main sources of the greenhouse problem. Some fuels contain more carbon than others and therefore generate more carbon dioxide when burned. Coal, for example, is higher in carbon than is oil, natural gas is relatively low, and synthetic fuels made from coal are highest. About half of the CO_2 generated by combustion of fossil fuels is absorbed by the oceans and in other natural processes; the remainder is added to the global atmosphere.[1] The rate of carbon dioxide emissions has been increasing throughout the twentieth century because of growing reliance on fossil fuels. Also, cutting down of the world's forests may have reduced a natural "sink" (an absorber) for carbon dioxide and thereby increased the amount that stays in the atmosphere.

In addition to CO_2, there are other atmospheric gases that trap heat radiated from the earth. The trace gases that deplete ozone also function as "greenhouse" gases; these include methane, fluorocarbons, and nitrous oxide (N_2O). Although less significant than these, there are numerous other trace gases. Some (including carbon tetrachloride and methyl chloroform) have direct heating effects; others (such as carbon monoxide and various hydrocarbons) have an indirect effect through chemical interactions with other atmospheric gases, especially ozone. Altogether, there are more than thirty gases other than carbon dioxide that may contribute to the greenhouse effect.[2]

Rate and magnitude of warming

Global warming currently is expected to be directly proportional to increases in atmospheric concentrations of the various greenhouse gases, and buildup of these gases is expected to be directly proportional to increased use of fossil fuels and the other activities discussed above. But how rapidly fossil fuel consumption accelerates is an economic issue, as are usage rates of nitrogen fertilizers, fluorocarbons, and most other greenhouse gases. Thus, there is no way to scientifically determine how soon climate changes will occur.

For most of the twentieth century, consumption of fossil fuel has increased about 4 percent annually, but since 1973 that rate has dropped by almost half. Analysts differ in their projections of future increases in use of fossil fuels; carbon emissions would double in about seventy years at a 1 percent rate of growth, in thirty-five years at a 2 percent rate, and in just over twenty-three years at a 3 percent rate.

Taking such uncertainties into account, a 1983 National Research Council report projected a doubling of atmospheric CO_2 shortly after 2065, but the report calculated that this could occur considerably sooner—or later. The odds given on each date were as follows:

Chances of CO_2 Doubling	Year
5 percent	by 2035
27 percent	by 2050
50 percent	by 2065
75 percent	by 2100

The NRC committee cautioned that "unless this uncertainty can be reduced by further research, it would appear to be unwise to dismiss the possibility that a CO_2 doubling may occur in the first half of the twenty-first century."[3]

The lowest temperature increase presently considered credible is 1.5°C for a doubling of preindustrial CO_2 levels; the highest is 4.5°C (Approximately 8°F). Figures in the lower half of the range are most commonly cited. Climate changes obviously will begin sooner and temperatures will go much higher in the long term if 4.5°C is correct.

Possible effects

Depending on how much warming occurs, the greenhouse effect could involve much more than just an increase in temperature. Significant changes could occur in regional climates, including shifts in precipitation patterns that would alter the location of fertile areas, marginal lands, and deserts.[4] Drier conditions would probably prevail over much of the western two-thirds of the United States and Canada, where most of the world's surplus grain now is produced. Presently fertile regions of the Soviet Union are also expected to suffer; but the Soviet Union has north-flowing rivers that could be diverted to replace local rainfall, so the USSR's northern regions might become more fertile if warmer temperatures bring a northward shift in the temperate zone. Areas of the Middle East also could benefit from the change in precipitation patterns, and many other places would be wetter, especially coastal areas.[5]

Whether a warmer world as a whole will be more or less able to feed a growing population is uncertain. Growing seasons obviously will be longer, but changes will be necessary in land use patterns and in the crops that can be grown in each climate region. Water shortages could lead to large-scale dislocations of the population, which would subsequently interfere with an orderly process of farming and require a reorientation of energy and resources that could stress even affluent nations; poor nations could encounter very serious difficulties.

A second major threat from the greenhouse effect is the possibility of widespread melting of ice in the polar regions. The most vulnerable area appears to be the West Antarctic ice sheet, which is grounded below sea level. If summer temperatures in the area increase by about 5°C, according to one research team, the ice sheet would be "vulnerable to rapid disintegration and melting . . . requiring a century or less and causing a sea level rise of five to six meters."[6] However, other scientists express doubts about the likelihood of such melting.

If melting should occur in polar regions, it would raise sea level in coastal regions of the United States anywhere from two to twelve feet, according to current estimates. This would flood one-fourth of Florida and Louisiana, one-tenth of New Jersey, and many other coastal lowlands throughout the world.[7] Millions of people might have to leave the heavily populated coastal areas where much of the world's agriculture and commerce takes place. Adjacent areas forced to accept such refugees from the coast would also be severely disrupted.

A report on CO_2 and energy use by President Carter's Council on Environmental Quality presented a combination of flooding and weather changes in a worst-case scenario:

> U.S. agricultural production declines sharply due to the extremely arid conditions prevalent over most of what were prime agricultural regions. Marginal agricultural areas in many arid and semi-arid regions of the world become unproductive, with particularly severe impacts on many less developed countries. Because of the rapidity of climate changes, other nations are unable quickly to take advantage of what might have been more favorable growing conditions—increased precipitation combined with higher temperatures and an extended growing season. Agricultural disruption causes widespread food shortages and hunger. Massive inflation occurs as the prices of declining quantities of basic crops rapidly increase. Migration out of climatically impoverished areas is restricted by political boundaries and cultural differences. Near the end of the twenty-first century, the West Antarctic ice sheet finally disintegrates, causing the sea level to rise some five to eight meters and coastal areas to flood.[8]

The Original Strategy: Reduction of Uncertainty

The principal strategy employed against the greenhouse effect has been to attempt to reduce uncertainty about the nature, magnitude, and timing of this threat by increased scientific efforts at research and monitoring.

Early scientific research

The first description of the greenhouse effect was given in 1863, at almost the same time that the technologies of the Industrial Revolution began to create the greenhouse problem. Tyndall, a British scientist, was the first to recognize that water vapor transmits to the earth a substantial portion of sunlight received in the upper atmosphere, while blocking infrared radiation from the earth that otherwise would escape back into space.[9] Because carbon dioxide molecules have the same radiation-transmitting properties as water vapor, scientists soon hypothesized that increased CO_2 would cause a warming of the earth's surface and the surrounding atmosphere because less heat could be reradiated into space. The Swedish scientist Arrhenius calculated in 1896 that a doubling of CO_2 would cause an increase of 6°C (11°F) in the mean annual global temperature.[10] In 1899 Chamberlin reached the same conclusion as a result of work on glaciation. "What caused glacial periods and warming periods?" he asked. His answer was: CO_2 fluctuations.[11]

Early in the twentieth century, several scholars perceived the importance of increasing fossil fuel combustion and suggested that dramatic increases in CO_2 might occur. Others, however, were concerned about possible diminution of atmospheric CO_2 due to a decline in volcanic activity. In 1938 Callendar, a British meteorologist, used recent measurements of global temperature changes to argue that the slight warming of the global atmosphere since the mid-1800s could be accounted for by increasing combustion of fossil fuels.[12] However, his case won few adherents.

As part of the postwar boom in scientific research, a number of U.S. scientists began in the 1950s to investigate the carbon cycle. A scientist at Ford Motor Company made the first sophisticated calculations of surface temperature responses to increased CO_2; he estimated a 3.6°C increase for doubled CO_2.[13] Enough research on the issue was underway by 1957 so that two scientists could confidently term CO_2 released by human activities a "large-scale geophysical experiment."[14]

In 1963 the Conservation Foundation sponsored a conference on this subject and brought it into wider public awareness.[15] This awareness grew when in 1965, the president's Science Advisory Committee cited the CO_2 problem as a potential threat to the Antarctic ice cap.[16]

In 1970 the MIT-based Study of Critical Environmental Problems joined the growing number of scientific organizations that had come to subscribe to the CO_2-warming hypothesis.[17] Then in 1971 the Study of Man's Impact on Climate drew scientists from all over the world to survey the state of knowledge in this field of study. This group of scientists put together detailed recommendations concerning the additional research and the CO_2 monitoring efforts necessary to confirm the extent of the threat and to improve overall understanding of the CO_2 cycle and its associated problems.[18] At about this time, the U.S. Committee for the Global Atmospheric Research Program also recommended a set of research priorities, as did the international Joint Organizing Committee of the same organization.[19] Among many other efforts in the ensuing decade, major international workshops were held in Germany in 1976 and 1977 to update research on CO_2.[20]

The U.S. government has been ahead of all others in fostering research and discussion on the greenhouse threat. Reports on the topic have been issued steadily since the early 1970s by numerous federal agencies and government-affiliated scientific organizations. Research expenditures as of 1984 were estimated at $20 million annually by the Office of Science and Technology Policy.[21] The Department of Energy has an entire division devoted to carbon dioxide research, and congressional committees have held hearings on the greenhouse issue since the mid-1970s.[22]

A consideration of the uncertainties

Researchers gradually identified major areas of uncertainty about the greenhouse effect, one of which is the fundamental question: will increases in atmospheric carbon dioxide actually lead to increases in temperature? The only way to know for sure is to detect confirming evidence that the world's climate actually is beginning to get warmer. Part of the research endeavor, therefore, has been devoted to the search for a "CO_2 signal."

Global temperature rose approximately 0.6°C (1°F) between 1880 and 1940. In the ensuing thirty years, temperatures declined by about 0.3°C. Then another warming trend set in about 1971, and global temperatures increased by 0.24°C just during the 1970s. Because of the cooling trend between 1940 and 1970, a number of scientists have questioned whether the temperature increase after 1970 was due to human activities.

They thought it might be due to changes in intensity of solar radiation, to dust particles from volcanic eruptions, and to other natural phenomena.

Fortunately, this type of question can be partially checked against experience. The measured increase in temperature generally corresponds with the climatic warming that contemporary scientific models calculate should have occurred over the past century due to use of fossil fuels and other greenhouse gases. For example, one group of researchers has attributed about 60 percent of the warming since 1970 to a 12 parts per million increase in atmospheric carbon dioxide. The remaining warming they believe to have been caused by other greenhouse gases.[23] So there is modest (but far from universal) scientific agreement that a warming effect is already occurring.

The extent of future warming remains in doubt, however, partly because of the overall imprecision of climate models. There are also specific uncertainties, such as whether the warming trend will create other effects that slow down the warming. Warmer, moister air may create denser clouds, for example, thereby screening out a portion of incoming solar radiation; according to one researcher, this could "reduce the expected warming over the next century by as much as one half."[24] There may be other feedback effects that magnify or speed up the warming trend.

Another key uncertainty concerns the changes in regional climate, especially rainfall, that would result from increases in temperature. Reconstructions of regional climate patterns using geological evidence from warmer periods partly confirm projected changes, but there still is a long way to go in refining scientific understanding of regional climate patterns. Moreover, it is not yet clear how changes in the amount of rainfall translate into changes in the amount of usable water; the common assumption is that stream runoff would diminish appreciably, but some water resource analysts predict just the opposite. Also, since more carbon dioxide in the air will enhance plant metabolism, there is a (yet to be confirmed) possibility that less water may be necessary for agriculture. However, leaves grown in laboratories under enriched carbon dioxide conditions have less protein, so insects tend to eat more, and therefore plant production "could even be reduced below current levels."[25]

Another element of uncertainty was identified in the mid-1970s when a number of scientists suggested that the cutting down of the world's forests could be decreasing natural consumption of CO_2 and thereby increasing the rate at which CO_2 is added to the atmosphere. Insects and bacteria would also add CO_2 to the atmosphere as they consumed the decaying vegetable matter remaining from deforestation. However, more recent studies have argued that forest regrowth has balanced cutting in recent years. While there still is some controversy on this point, most researchers believe that combustion of fossil fuels will be the only major factor in future changes in atmospheric CO_2 levels.[26]

Still another area of uncertainty concerns the contribution of gases other than carbon dioxide to the greenhouse effect. It was not until the late 1970s that scientists directed systematic attention to the potential greenhouse effects of methane, nitrous oxide, and other trace gases. Even up to 1985 these gases had received considerably less attention than CO_2. In spite of the NRC's recognition that controlling emissions of other trace gases may be cheaper and easier than controlling emissions of carbon dioxide, less than ten pages in their five hundred-page 1983 report were devoted to this matter.

Atmospheric methane concentrations have increased substantially over the past several centuries and could double by the year 2050. This would contribute about 0.2°C to global warming.[27] The rate of methane released is almost certain to go up, since much of it occurs during production of important food sources. Moreover, increased carbon *mon*oxide in the lower atmosphere will reduce the concentration of compounds that destroy methane, and as global warming occurs, extensive peat bogs in northern latitudes may thaw and release huge quantities of trapped methane. Also possible are methane releases from continental slope marine sediments.[28]

The effects on global temperature of fluorocarbons are difficult to predict. In one study, these chemicals were projected to contribute to an eventual temperature increase of 0.3°C if their production remained at 1973 levels.[29] Because of the ozone controversy and sluggish economic growth, usage of fluorocarbons dropped until 1983, when it began to rise rapidly. Production increases of 3 to 5 percent annually are considered possible but not certain. Moreover, as described in chapter 5, the distribution of ozone at different altitudes is changing, in part because of fluorocarbons. Because the effects of ozone on surface temperature vary at different altitudes, the overall effects of fluorocarbons on climate are very complex.

By 1985 the most comprehensive study on the combined effects of all the greenhouse gases concluded that the effects of the other trace gases "are as important as that of CO_2 increase in determining the climate change of the future or the past one hundred years." This group of researchers calculated a 0.8°C (1.4°F) warming due to trace gases by 2030.[30] But another prominent scientist, who chaired the National Research Council's 1983 study, countered that he "would be inclined to take [these results] with a grain of salt. You're on surer ground with CO_2."[31] It is thus evident that there is not yet agreement on the scientific issues involved in the effects of trace gases and even less consensus about future rates of increase in their production and use.

Another uncertainty about the warming effect concerns the probability and extent of flooding due to melting polar ice. There is disagreement about the extent of warming in the southern hemisphere. Some researchers claim that warming in the Antarctic will approximate the global mean; if this is correct, not much melting would occur. A majority of researchers, however, expect that warming at the poles will be more than twice the global average; this could cause major melting.[32] Moreover, current theories cannot predict whether the land-based Greenland and East Antarctic ice sheets would shrink or grow with a warmer climate. If the ocean warms while the air above the ice sheets remains below freezing, for example, increased snowfall could enlarge these icecaps, with a consequent *reduction* in sea level.

By the mid-1980s, then, a pluralistic process of research and monitoring by diverse groups of scientists had highlighted the (large) remaining uncertainties about the greenhouse threat. Despite substantial improvements in meteorology and other relevant sciences, however, relatively little progress was made in actually reducing the uncertainties about the timing, magnitude, and effects of the projected climate changes.

Need for more focused research and monitoring

Identification of the above-mentioned uncertainties has made them, to some extent, the focus of greenhouse effect research. But since the number of potentially useful research projects on this topic is so large, some way to set priorities is necessary. Congress suggested one approach for priority setting in the Energy Security Act of 1980. Because the synthetic fuels industry (which this law sought to establish) would contribute to the greenhouse threat, Congress directed the Office of Science and Technology Policy to coordinate with the National Research Council to comprehensively study the carbon dioxide problem.[33] Congress asked that the following issues be addressed:

A comprehensive assessment of CO_2 releases and impacts;

Advice on how to structure a long-term program of domestic and international CO_2 research and assessment, including definition of the U.S. role and the necessary financial resources;

Evaluation of "how the ongoing United States government carbon dioxide assessment program should be modified so as to be of increased utility in providing information and recommendations of the highest possible value to government policy makers."[34]

Through a newly formed Carbon Dioxide Assessment Committee, the NRC issued a 1983 report generally considered to be a very good overview of the greenhouse threat.[35] But the NRC fully addressed only the first of the tasks that Congress posed (namely, comprehensive assessment). No attention was devoted to the third item, and instead of analyzing the structure of an international research program (as suggested in the second item), the committee merely constructed a very long list of the research topics it considered desirable to pursue. Among some one hundred topics were the following:

Long-range economic and energy simulation models for projecting CO_2 emissions;

Studies of ice cores, tree rings, and lake sediments to refine historical knowledge on past CO_2 concentrations;

More sophisticated ocean modeling, to better predict rates of CO_2 uptake and warming of various ocean layers;

Modeling and data collection on cloudiness;

Sediment sampling programs on continental slopes to learn more about vast quantities of trapped methane that could be released as oceans get warmer;

A wide variety of studies of the Antarctic ice sheet;

Effects of carbon dioxide on photosynthesis and plant growth;

Climatic effects on agricultural pests;

Possible human health risks from higher CO_2 levels;

Extensive water conservation research.

In addition to research on the carbon cycle, the NRC committee called for more extensive and more sophisticated monitoring to determine more conclusively whether climatic changes actually are beginning to occur. As one part of the NRC report put it, "Policy makers are not likely to take action unless we can demonstrate that CO_2 actually is making the climate warmer."[36] Among the types of monitoring called for by the NRC were:

Expanded, ongoing temperature measurement to detect a CO_2 "signal" at the earliest possible date;

Systematic, ongoing oceanic measurements throughout the world from research ships, ocean-scanning satellites, and other sources;

Improved monitoring of non-CO_2 greenhouse gases.

No doubt these all are worthwhile measures to extend scientific understanding, with or without a greenhouse problem. But this leaves us with a long list of research topics and with little prospect of quickly narrowing the uncertainties. Are some uncertainties more important than others? Is there a subset of research topics that would allow policy makers to come more quickly to an understanding of the issues? For example, it is likely that some of the trace gases deserve more attention than others. It is known that some of these gases will be easier to limit than others, so it is sensible to invest scientific resources where there is more potential for control. Since each gas reflects back to earth only certain wavelengths of escaping heat radiation, moreover, some "windows" may be of greater concern than others. For example, gases that reflect on approximately the same wavelength as carbon dioxide may not result in as much additional climatic warming as gases that block other windows. If so, then both research and control strategies might focus on the especially troublesome gases.[37]

These are the kinds of priorities that must be established and addressed before policy makers can begin to act. The failure to date to establish realistic research priorities based on the need of policy makers is a significant shortcoming in the strategy deployed against the greenhouse effect.

Alternative Intervention Strategies

If and when the uncertainties about the greenhouse effect are reduced and agreement to act against this threat is reached, what control strategies are available? At least four are already under discussion among scientists and policy analysts.

Promoting alternatives to risky activities

The most obvious strategy would be to examine safer ways to accomplish those economic functions that now are creating the greenhouse effect. It is debatable whether this is a practicable approach. To pursue it would require aggressive energy conservation and substantial increases in research and development on nonfossil energy sources. Solar and biomass energy sources are usually envisioned, but greater reliance on nuclear power might also be included.

Some energy analysts believe that strategy should be initiated at once, not only to reduce the greenhouse threat, but also to reduce reliance on foreign oil and limit acid rain. Others see the conservation/alternative fuels option more as a backup strategy; as the 1983 NRC committee expressed it: "We may find that emissions are rising rapidly, that the fraction remaining airborne is high, that climate is very sensitive to CO_2 increase, or that the impacts of climate change are costly and divisive. In such a case, we want to have an enhanced ability to make a transition to nonfossil fuels."[38]

Most energy analysts expect continuing improvements in energy efficiency and alternative energy availability, but the view held by many is that increases in demand for energy will outstrip such improvements. The NRC 1983 report, for example, estimated that world fossil fuel consumption would approximately triple by the year 2100 in the absence of major bans, taxes, or other disruptions of consumption. But the Harvard Energy Policy Project and some scenarios from the International Institute for Applied Systems Analysis are more optimistic about the potential for replacing fossil energy sources with renewable ones.[39] A 1984 Stanford/MIT study calculated that changing patterns of energy usage from fossil fuels to other existing technologies by just 1 percent per year would reduce climatic warming greatly and extend it over a much longer period at reasonable costs.[40]

It is worth recalling, moreover, that as recently as 1975—after the initial OPEC oil embargo—most analysts overestimated the U.S. energy demand for 1985 by more than 50 percent. If this much error can occur in ten years, current projections for the years 2050 or 2100 could be even more flawed.[41] Thus, the feasibility of this conservation/renewable energy strategy is debatable but not clearly disproven.

Limiting dangerous activity

If the conservation/renewable energy strategy is not sufficient, an obvious supplement to this strategy would be to limit risky activities in some way. This was the strategy followed in restricting the amount of pesticide residue on fruit, the quantity of air pollutants released from a factory, and regulations of numerous other health and safety threats. In the greenhouse effect case, this strategy could result in limiting the amount or type of fossil fuel burned each year as well as limiting use of other greenhouse gases. At least two tactics—taxes and bans—can be used in implementing this strategy.

As recent successes in energy conservation demonstrate, one way to reduce the use of fossil fuels is to increase their price. This will occur to some extent as a result of supply and demand for depletable resources, but prices could be increased even more by levying a tax. For example, EPA has investigated the following option that would double the cost of shale oil, a (future) fuel high in carbon:[42]

Fuel	Tax Percent
Shale oil	100
Synthetic gas (from coal)	86
Synthetic oil (from coal)	81
Coal	52
Conventional oil	41
Conventional gas	29
Unconventional gas	29
Solar, biomass, hydro	0

Lower carbon fuels would be taxed in proportion to their carbon content.

How much effect would levying such taxes have on reducing use? The only way to judge this is to rely on an economic model that forecasts future energy usage via computer simulation, and no such model has a record of demonstrated reliability.[43] However, one well-regarded model used by EPA predicts that such a tax applied worldwide would reduce CO_2 emissions by some 18 percent by the year 2050 and by 42 percent by the year 2100.[44] This would reduce global temperature by 0.7°C by the year 2100, if global warming is on the low end of the anticipated range; if warming is greater, the reduction would be greater. Higher taxes would lead to greater temperature reduction; a tax imposed only in the United States would have about one-third the effect of a world tax.[45]

An even more stringent approach would be to ban the use of high-carbon fuels. As a result, solid fuel prices would more than double due to scarcity and total demand for energy would drop by about 50 percent. A major shift to cultivation of plants for both solid and liquid fuels would be expected, and this form of biomass energy does not add increased carbon dioxide to the atmosphere. As a result, projected CO_2 emissions for the year 2100 could be cut about in half by a ban on coal or shale oil. If both were banned, CO_2 emissions could be reduced substantially from their present level according to EPA calculations. Banning both would delay the projected date that CO_2 would double by about twenty-five years and would cut almost in half the overall temperature increase by the year 2100.[46]

The drawback of these particular strategies is that they would be very costly. Banning coal or heavily taxing its use would have massive negative economic consequences that perhaps would rival the impact of the greenhouse effect itself. The likelihood that such measures would be implemented even in the United States, let alone in other nations with fewer energy alternatives, is small.

Partial bans or taxes could be applied to some of the other greenhouse gases. Taxes to increase the price of such gases presumably would cut usage. Limits on authorized production levels, such as those used for fluorocarbons in Europe, might be a simpler way to achieve the same outcome. How much of an effect could be achieved at what cost is even more of an unknown for these other trace gases than for CO_2. Yet production of some of these gases is growing rapidly, and they could have as much influence on climate as carbon dioxide. So serious attention to control strategies appears overdue.

Preventing dangers

The strategies discussed above rely on limiting risky activities, such as fossil fuel combustion. An alternative strategy would be to allow these activities to continue but to make them safer, and some analysts believe that it may be possible to prevent fossil fuel combustion from leading to the greenhouse effect. For example, one suggestion in 1977 was to install "scrubbers" (equipment for removing carbon dioxide) on coal-fired power plants; the captured CO_2 would be injected deep into the ocean.[47] The technical obstacles to this approach are probably insurmountable, but the underlying goal is worth pursuing.

One tactic would focus on long-term removal of carbon dioxide from the atmosphere. Because trees metabolyze carbon dioxide and incorporate the carbon into their fibers, it is conceivable that enough trees could be planted to significantly reduce the amount of CO_2 in the atmosphere. The idea of using forests as a sink for CO_2 emerged in the mid-1970s when concerns arose about the effects of deforestation.[48] Such a reforestation effort would build up the quality of soils and help prevent erosion besides being aesthetically appealing. Moreover, as a decentralized solution to a global problem, it is politically attractive.

Unfortunately, the obstacles to this approach are severe. If American sycamores were used because they grow well in temperate climates with minimal rainfall, one analysis estimated that a land area roughly the size of Europe would be required to offset fifty years of carbon dioxide emissions (at current, not increased, rates).[49] Enormous quantities of fertilizer would be required. Acreage requirements would be reduced substantially by using a tropical tree such as the Hawaiian leucaena, which absorbs four times as much carbon, but irrigation and fertilizer requirements would increase substantially. A 1983 EPA estimate put the initial cost as high as $400 billion, with annual expenses perhaps reaching $100 billion.[50]

As large as this sum is, it is a small percentage of worldwide energy expenses, and there would be offsetting revenues from harvesting such forests. A recent EPA study nevertheless concluded that "sequestering atmospheric CO_2 by trees is an extremely expensive, essentially infeasible option for controlling CO_2."[51] While obviously expensive, reforestation could actually prove to be a bargain in comparison with other alternatives such as banning the use of coal.

Another approach to preventing the greenhouse threat (at this stage no more than speculation) would be to actively intervene in the atmosphere to offset the warming trend. Several scientists have suggested injecting sulfur dioxide into the stratosphere to reflect a portion of incoming sunlight, but costs and environmental effects (such as acid rain) would have to be carefully examined.[52] Alternatively, temporary cooling results naturally from the enormous quantities of dust spewed into the atmosphere by major volcanic eruptions. Would deliberate injection of dust particles into the atmosphere be technically feasible? If so, would it be relatively benign environmentally? There has not been extended study of such corrective options, and, while all such possibilities might prove infeasible or even highly dangerous, they deserve careful scrutiny.

Mitigating the effects

Another possibility, perhaps the most popular at present, is simply to live with the effects of a warmer climate. After all, humans are extremely adaptable and already live with climate variations much greater than those that can be expected from the greenhouse effect. The changes will be phased in over a half century or so, and there will be considerable time to make necessary adjustments. Some observers see this as a more-or-less automatic process, while others believe that we should begin now to develop tactics for mitigating undesired effects.[53]

What would be required to prepare for a drier climate? Especially in the midwestern and western United States, a small change in rainfall and runoff could lead to a large change in agricultural productivity unless adaptive measures are taken. While a fair amount is known about water conservation and re-use measures, a great deal more can be learned. Because planning the distribution of water for entire river basins requires a long lead time, the NRC has suggested that necessary research and modifications of water use begin in the near future. Ways to cope with a warmer climate might include: breeding genetic strains of crops that grow well in warmer and drier climates with higher CO_2 levels, stockpiling larger quantities of agricultural stocks to guard against famine, producing food in factories through methods such as fermentation, and farming in massive plastic greenhouses to conserve water.

Possible increase in sea level is another matter of concern. Hazardous waste dumps need to be located well out of the path of rising waters, and major new construction in coastal areas should have a relatively short coastal exposure and a sufficiently high proportion of valuable activities so that funds will be available for construction and maintenance of sea walls. Some research and development, on improved seawall construction for example, would also be necessary. Given the generally poor record for urban and regional planning, new federal laws may be required.

None of the above options have been examined in any detail, and no serious cost analyses have been attempted. The widespread assumption—and it is only an assumption—is that such measures would be less expensive than prevention of CO_2 buildup. As one prominent climatologist who advocates these and other adaptive strategies admits: "What can be done to prevent a tragedy of Dust Bowl proportions? The strategies are not entirely clear."[54] So while the possibility of simply living with the greenhouse effect is an interesting option, its costs and benefits remain to be clarified.

Appraising the Current Strategy

The primary strategy employed to date against the greenhouse threat has been to employ a diverse number of physical scientists to study the risks. This research-and-monitoring approach is likely to remain the central strategy for the foreseeable future, with the goal of reducing the substantial uncertainties about the impact of the greenhouse threat. If agreement is reached on the need to take action, at least four strategies may be available:

Reducing the need for the risky activity by energy conservation, emphasizing nonfossil fuels, or finding safer alternatives to greenhouse gases;

Restricting the risky activity by fuel taxes, production quotas for greenhouse gases, or selective bans on high-carbon fossil fuels;

Making the activities less risky, for instance, by offsetting the effects of fossil fuel use by reforestation;

Mitigating the effects of climate changes by altering patterns of agriculture, water use, and other activities likely to be affected.

Decisions about whether or when to employ these measures apparently are to be deferred pending further clarification of the greenhouse threat. What are the strengths and weaknesses of such attempts at clarification?

The research-and-monitoring system

The routes for focusing scientific attention in the greenhouse case were almost identical to those used in the ozone case. Early investigators conducted basic research on the atmosphere, glaciation, and other natural phenomena long before a greenhouse problem was suspected. As scientific knowledge gradually grew, scientists' concerns stimulated some government officials to increase funds for atmospheric research. This resulted in further improvements in the relevant sciences, together with authoritative reports on the subject of the possible greenhouse effect. These reports then became media events, which heightened public awareness and led to additional concern in Congress.

Four subcomponents of this process—ordinarily taken for granted by those who participate in the process—are important elements in an overall strategy that society has evolved for diagnosing potential catastrophe. First, a large and complex problem was broken down into many smaller, more comprehensible parts. For instance, glaciologists studied core samples of ice from Greenland to determine carbon dioxide levels thousands of years ago and used special dating and testing mechanisms developed by still other scientific specialists.[55]

Second, diverse subgroups of researchers competed to define the nature and extent of the problem. For example, computer simulations of climate by atmospheric chemists competed with interpretations of past geological experience. Oceanographers and atmospheric chemists attempted in very different ways to determine the percentage of released CO_2 that is absorbed into the oceans as compared with the atmosphere. Even within subfields, scientists at different universities and in different nations developed unique sets of data and approaches to interpreting such data.

Third, these disparate viewpoints are taken into account and to some degree reconciled by a standard process. One part of it is the normal scientific process: some ideas become dominant because they are more persuasive than the competing ones. In addition, when a major scientific organization such as the National Research Council produces a report, it typically gains the attention of media, policy makers, and the scientific community. The expressed view may be widely persuasive and lead to consensus, or it may be controversial and provide other scientists and policy analysts with a target against which to react in formulating their own versions of the situation. In the greenhouse case, such major committee reports contributed to a broader perspective than would the isolated work of individual scientists or policy analysts.

Fourth, government agencies typically commission further studies, which emphasize explicit policy concerns and help focus policy makers' attention on an issue. The EPA's controversial 1983 report, disavowed by the Reagan Administration, was the prime example to date in the greenhouse case. Its title clearly indicates the change in emphasis: "Can We Delay a Greenhouse Warming?"

Obstacles to implementing a strategy

The research-and-monitoring system described above is an effective method that will almost automatically diagnose threats to society from a variety of risky technologies. But diagnosis is only a first step; once the risk is perceived, further steps must be taken to guard against the worst possible outcome. These further steps have been taken for every other risky technology reviewed in this volume, but to date this has not occurred for the greenhouse problem. While it may be too early to expect action, we suspect that there are fundamental obstacles to effective action on this issue in the foreseeable future.

One of the largest obstacles is the ambiguity about whether the greenhouse effect would on balance be positive or negative. This ambiguity is not characteristic of any other risky technology reviewed in this volume (with the possible exception of the warm water released by nuclear power plants). Because some regions will benefit by the resulting changes in climate and precipitation patterns, the international agreement necessary to substantially reduce the greenhouse problem is difficult to achieve. Thus, the very nature of the greenhouse problem may prevent effective action to avert anticipated threats.

Another drawback in addressing this problem is the inability of scientists to narrow the remaining disagreements about the carbon dioxide controversy in a way that will enable policy makers to make decisions. While there is a working consensus among scientists regarding a buildup of carbon dioxide and other greenhouse chemicals, there is disagreement about how soon this will occur and how severe the effects will be. The range of uncertainty may render these calculations useless to policy makers. For instance, while the lower estimate of a 1.5°C rise in mean global temperature might be widely acceptable (given the high costs of averting it), the highest credible estimated increase of 4.5°C probably would be intolerable to the majority of policy makers. So unless scientists can pinpoint the risks more precisely, their findings may have little effect on policy. Yet in the period from 1979 through 1985 when investigations of the greenhouse effect probably tripled all previous research, virtually no progress was made in narrowing this range of uncertainty.[56]

Given the potential risks, it is still reasonable to attempt to reduce remaining uncertainties through continued research and monitoring, but it is not clear how to proceed. The NRC provided a long list of research issues requiring further attention, but it did not convey which, if any, questions were truly pivotal. Nor did it attempt to define the critical variables or uncertainties or to set priorities among research topics. What is necessary is not just more knowledge, but knowledge that will make a difference to government policy. Much more attention should be paid now to setting priorities for the research-and-monitoring system.

Another difficulty concerns the costs of action. While sustained research has been directed at illuminating the causes, timing, and magnitude of the greenhouse effect, much less effort has been expended in exploring possible actions to be taken in response to the anticipated problems. Whether to initiate action depends in large part on the costs of initiating action now versus the costs of postponing it. The policy sections of greenhouse studies typically assume—in the absence of more compelling evidence—that the costs of action are too large to justify policy changes. Most of the actions proposed so far would in fact be extremely costly, but too little attention has been given to searching for practical options.

For instance, there might be combinations of partial solutions that would keep costs bearable and also at least slow the increase of greenhouse gases. For example, an easing of the problem might be achieved by carefully researching how to adapt to temperature increases while at the same time limiting use of high-carbon fuels and instituting a partial reforestation program. So far, little effort has been made to explore such pragmatic solutions either in a national or international framework. The longer actions are delayed the more severe they may ultimately have to be.

Similarly, little effort has been devoted to studying the magnitude and timing of preventive actions. For example, if temperature increases are at the low end of the expected range, how long can we wait before taking action? On the other hand, if increases are at the high end, how much longer can we safely afford to wait?

Whatever information is obtained about costs and other aspects of the greenhouse effect, this will not automatically lead to a decision. Judgments about how much protection is desirable—costs versus risks—will still need to be made. In the cases of toxic chemicals and nuclear power, decision makers sometimes chose to err on the side of safety—they moved ahead more slowly or designed more stringently than might have been strictly necessary. The equivalent approach in the greenhouse case would be to take initial steps to reduce or offset emissions of fossil fuels or greenhouse gases, even without conclusive evidence about the risks. But how soon would be soon enough to take such initial steps? Research and monitoring will not aid such a decision because there still remain conflicts over values.

One group of conservation/renewable energy advocates argues for action now:

> To postpone action until climatic change is detected entails the risk of being unable to prevent further harmful changes that could prove irreversible for centuries.
>   . . . [Moreover] gradual changes are almost always more easily accomodated, in terms of both economic and social costs, than precipitous changes. . . . A lower growth rate of fossil fuel use over the next few decades, combined with a more efficient use of energy, would reduce the pressures for rapid societal and technological change later on and allow more time for development of alternative energy sources. Conversely, a more rapid increase in fossil fuel use during the next decade might necessitate an earlier and more drastic reduction.[57]

In contrast, the NRC assessment committee was distinctly cool toward near-term action, as indicated in their 1983 report:

> The potential disruptions associated with CO_2-induced climatic change are sufficiently serious to make us lean away from fossil fuel energy options, if other things are equal. However, our current assessment . . . justifies primarily increased monitoring and vigilance and not immediate action to curtail fossil fuel use.[58]

But this conclusion was based in part on scientific interpretations subsequently called into question. In particular, an important 1985 study reported the possibility that "most of the expected warming attributable to [already released] trace gases probably has not yet occurred." If there is a long delay before the earth's temperature fully adjusts to atmospheric changes, the scientists said, "this calls into question a policy of 'wait and see.' "[59] Changes may be necessary now, for twenty-first-century changes in fossil fuel combustion and trace gas emissions might come too late to have much effect on climate until the following century.

The "How soon to act?" question is reminiscent of the "How safe?" issue that has plagued regulation of nuclear power. How conservative should society be in the face of gross factual uncertainties about the likelihood and magnitude of a technological danger? Waiting to act entails some risk; delay is not the most cautious action. Is waiting nevertheless justified? Are the risks of delay worth such benefits as minimizing economic repercussions or acquiring further information? There is no scientific answer to this question; it requires instead a political judgment. And once action is initiated (if it is), policy makers on the greenhouse problem will then be faced with the same question confronting nuclear power regulators: namely, how far should one go in protecting against possible risks?

We will have more to say about the "How safe?—How soon?" question and about the costs of averting catastrophe in the concluding chapter.

7

A System
for Averting
Catastrophe

This volume began with an apparent paradox. We are surrounded by potentially catastrophic threats from civilian technologies and yet there has been no catastrophe. To what do we owe our good fortune? In examining five types of technological risks that pose a potential for catastrophe, it appears that our good fortune was due in part to luck, in part to delayed consequences yet to be faced, and in part to jerry-rigged solutions. A not insignificant part of the explanation, however, is that regulators have coped with risky technologies in a surprisingly intelligent manner. That is not to say that the outcomes are fully satisfactory; nonetheless, each risk has been approached using one or more sensible strategies. Moreover, the individual strategies at times cohere well enough to seem almost like a system.

The Strategies Now in Use

Use of toxic substances originally proceeded by trial and error, and chemicals were regulated only after negative consequences became apparent. This type of decision process is a well-known, thoroughly analyzed strategy for coping with complex problems (see the third section in this chapter). But we had assumed that long delays before obtaining feedback, coupled with severe consequences of error, would make trial and error inappropriate for managing hazardous chemicals. Contrary to our expectations, there proved to be numerous ways to obtain feedback about the effects of chemicals, as demonstrated in the case of pesticides, and regulators were able to take repeated corrective action in response to this feedback.

In the past several decades, however, the number of chemicals introduced into the environment and the number of people exposed to them has increased exponentially. The strategy of waiting to experience effects before taking action became less acceptable, and more deliberate steps were initiated. Two basic approaches evolved, both intended to prevent or reduce severe health and environmental consequences. First, new chemicals must now undergo a premanufacture notification and screening process that attempts to identify the most hazardous substances before they are marketed. Second, because the sheer number of existing chemicals prevents attention to all, priority-setting procedures identify those chemicals that most need testing and regulation.

In contrast to the case of toxic substances, regulation of nuclear power was never based on normal trial and error, even in its earliest days. The potential consequences of errors in design, construction, and operation were obviously unacceptable, yet the complexity of reactor designs made errors unavoidable. Nuclear regulators seem to have been aware of this dilemma from the early days of reactor development; their solution was, and still is, to attempt to make reactors forgiving of errors. They assumed that errors would occur and required that reactors be designed to withstand such errors. First, reactors were designed conservatively to *prevent* errors in design, construction, and operation from leading to a release of fission products from the core. This was achieved through wide margins for error, redundancies, and emergency systems. Second, reactors were designed to *minimize* the effects of accidents should they occur despite the attempts to prevent them. The main tactic to achieve this was containment. Over time, the primary emphasis in regulation has shifted to preventing core melts, and away from minimizing their effects.

The approach employed by the National Institutes of Health in regulating recombinant DNA research combined the strategies used for regulating nuclear power and toxic chemicals. On the one hand, an effort was made to make rDNA research forgiving of errors. Both physical and biological containment were required, so that if an organism were released during an experiment, it would be very unlikely to escape from the lab and establish itself in the environment. Having ensured protection from the consequences of error, policy makers then proceeded by trial and error. They initially established relatively stringent regulations—prohibiting six classes of experiments and requiring all others to be performed under varying degrees of containment. Gradually, as experience in recombinant DNA research grew, more experiments were allowed at lower levels of containment. Eventually, all the prohibitions and most of the containment requirements were dropped.

Some critics suspect that the NIH and the scientific community have been dishonest or biased about the risks associated with rDNA research. We find their arguments unpersuasive; but even if they are correct, the *strategy* that evolved for dealing with the rDNA problem was well suited to the nature of the problem that faced the NIH in the 1970s. In fact, it was identical to the strategy of nuclear decision makers in establishing their first regulatory policies. Instead of being relaxed over time, however, nuclear regulations gradually have been tightened. In our view, the difference in the fates of rDNA research and nuclear power is due to differences in the natures of the two problems. The risks of rDNA research were inherently more containable and more testable than those of nuclear power.

The ozone and greenhouse cases exhibit another pattern for averting catastrophe. In contrast to nuclear power and rDNA, no one suspected at the outset that there would be any harmful effects to the atmosphere. Thus, chemicals that deplete the ozone layer were released and fossil fuels were burned for many years before the possible problems were recognized. In contrast to toxic chemicals, the more diffused and subtle nature of the atmospheric threats prevented negative feedback from serving as a warning. Instead, some scientists predicted errors on the basis of scientific theories and atmosphere-climate computer simulation models. These scientists made their findings public, which led to media coverage and scrutiny by fellow scientists. These public revelations stimulated inquiry and funding of research by government and led to further scientific analysis of the threats.

Regulatory actions against atmospheric threats are even more difficult to devise than those for other risky technologies. Because ozone depletion and climatic warming are global phenomena, containment of the hazard is impossible, and only limited testing is practical. Furthermore, no one nation can do much to reduce the hazards, yet not all nations have the same incentive to act. So cooperative international action, while required, is improbable.

In the ozone case, the United States banned two of the major threats that seemed to pose the greatest risk with the fewest benefits: the SST and fluorocarbon aerosols. The implicit strategy was to take partial, readily available, and relatively low-cost steps to protect against the potential hazard. More extensive (and therefore more costly) actions were delayed until uncertainty about the likelihood and severity of the problem could be reduced through further scientific monitoring. Few other nations adopted this approach, and even the United States did not take action against other ozone depletion threats. As a result, the total quantity of ozone depleters released worldwide is now as high as it was at the height of the ozone controversy. Fortunately, it appears that other atmospheric phenomena at least partially offset this problem. The extent of the projected damage is still in dispute, but it may be somewhat less than originally expected.

No nation has yet taken action (beyond research) against the greenhouse threat. Such action would face many of the same obstacles confronted by efforts to stem ozone depletion. Moreover, the threat of climatic warming is a result largely of activities that are fundamental to a highly populated, affluent civilization. So while there are policy options available (such as reforestation or a coal ban) to counteract the greenhouse threat, these would be very expensive and politically unattractive. Mitigating the worst possible effects (for instance, through crop research) is the least expensive option in the short term, and therefore the most politically feasible.

Toward a Catastrophe-Aversion System

What do the five cases studied in this volume imply for the overall goal of averting catastrophes? Political scientist Todd LaPorte has noted that regulators of many risky technologies must strive for freedom from error; this has been nearly achieved in air traffic control.[1] He cautions that the training, design, and other requirements for error-free operation of risky technologies will be difficult to achieve. We go further than LaPorte in perceiving obstacles to error-free risk management. Except for a very few special cases where nearly complete information is available and the possible ways to err are limited, errors are unavoidable in the management of complex technologies. Air traffic control is one of the exceptions to this and not a model that can be applied generally. In the cases we have studied, freedom from error is not a realistic goal. The nature of potential errors is too uncertain, especially at the outset, to expect to prevent them all. It is this high degree of uncertainty, combined with the potential for catastrophe, that makes the cases so problematic. Errors cannot be avoided, yet errors can lead to catastrophe.

The strategies we found for coping with this dilemma were not fully developed, nor always implemented effectively. However, taken together they suggest the elements of a complete catastrophe-aversion system. The system is by no means mature, and it is never complete in any of our five cases. But the general structure can be discerned fairly readily and unambiguously.

Strategy 1: Protect against the potential hazard

If errors are inevitable and can lead to catastrophe, then the first priority is to protect against the worst consequences that might result from errors. We found five interrelated types of tactics for accomplishing this goal.

Containment of the effects of what might otherwise be a catastrophic accident was employed in the early nuclear and recombinant DNA research cases. In both cases, regulators believed that containment would make acceptable what otherwise could be serious accidents. When it can be achieved, this is the ideal solution to the dilemma. In effect, it eliminates the potential for catastrophe. Unfortunately, as we have seen, this goal usually is unattainable.[2] In the atmospheric cases, misguided policies can result in uncontainable global climate changes; use of toxic substances is too widely dispersed to allow for containment. And if containment is feasible at all for large conventional nuclear reactors, the cost would be prohibitive.

The safest (and costliest) alternative to containment is to prevent errors entirely by prohibiting the action or technology that poses the potential for uncontainable catastrophe. A less drastic measure is to impose a selective ban on risky technologies—such as the screening of toxic chemicals, early prohibitions on certain classes of rDNA experiments, and the elimination of most fluorocarbon aerosols. A still weaker variation of this strategy is to limit use of the technology to levels that are presumed to be safe or safer. One example of a way to head off the greenhouse effect would be to limit the amount of high-carbon fuels that can be burned. Another example, proposed but not implemented by EPA, would be to limit the amount of ozone-depleting chemicals that can be manufactured. The equivalent strategy applied to nuclear reactors would be to limit the size of reactors, their number, or the geographical areas in which they could be built.

Another tactic for protecting against potential hazards is to assume that errors will occur and take steps to prevent those errors from resulting in hazardous outcomes. This tactic was emphasized for reactors built after 1966, when errors still were inevitable but containment was no longer considered guaranteed. Substantially upgraded emergency core cooling systems, for example, were used in an effort to prevent reactor coolant leaks from triggering core melts. Another example of this tactic would be to attempt to offset the effects of CO_2 emissions by such measures as reforestation. This approach does not rely

Table 1   Strategy One: Protecting Against Potential Hazards

	Toxics	Nuclear	rDNA	Ozone	Greenhouse
Error					
Prohibition	X		X	X	
Limits on use	X			X	X
Prevention		X			X
Containment		X	X		
Mitigation		X			X
Catastrophe					

on the dubious hope of preventing all errors (although efforts are made to avoid them) but instead emphasizes preventing the effects of errors from producing a hazardous outcome; the point is to intervene in the sequence of events between error and severe consequence.

A final tactic is to assume that errors will occur and will trigger hazardous outcomes but to take steps that acceptably mitigate the impact. Many observers believe that this will work with the greenhouse effect because humans will adapt to a warmer and drier climate. Other examples of this tactic include remote siting of reactors (in the early nuclear era) and the proposed use of potassium iodide pills to prevent cancer of the thyroid in the event of a nuclear power plant accident. However, mitigation of effects is usually a supplemental strategy, not a primary method for averting catastrophe.

Table 1 summarizes the strategies for protecting against potential hazards used in these cases. It reveals that there are a number of points along the chain of events between error and catastrophe where regulators can intervene in order to protect against the catastrophe. At one end of the chain is the zero-risk option: prohibit the use of the risky technology. At the other end is catastrophe mitigation: the accident occurs and steps are taken to reduce its effects. Typically, prohibition is impractical and mitigation is incomplete. Some combination of the three intermediate strategies thus becomes necessary.

Strategy 2: Proceed cautiously

We rarely know in advance just how bad or how likely a hazard might be. On what basis, then, can policy makers decide whether to make protective measures tight, lax, or somewhere in between? Some strategy is required. In protecting against a potentially catastrophic threat, the second strategy is to err on the side of caution.

The nuclear case provides several illustrations of this approach. Early on, when reliance was placed on containment, acceptable reactor designs were based on judgments of whether the containment building could withstand the maximum credible accident. It would have been possible to be less cautious and to require that containment designs withstand only the most likely accidents. Instead, a more conservative approach was taken: assume the worst and design to withstand it. Similarly, reactors were required to withstand higher than likely temperatures and pressures and were built with several levels of redundancies. Even the redundant systems—such as the emergency core cooling system—were designed to withstand higher than expected temperatures and pressures. Since caution is a matter of degree, some critics of nuclear power argue that decision makers should have been even more cautious.

Another important element of a cautious strategy is how the burden of proof is determined and on whom it falls. At one extreme, new technical activities could be considered dangerous until proven otherwise. Even faint suspicions of danger would be adequate reason to withhold approval, and the burden of proving safety would rest entirely on the party seeking to undertake the activity. This was the case with recombinant DNA research in the mid-1970s when elaborate and stringent precautions were taken. At the other extreme (approached earlier in this century), new activities would be considered safe until proven dangerous. The government would be required to prove danger, and only compelling evidence would be sufficient to slow or stop a technical activity. Over the past decades, the burden of proof has shifted significantly toward the proponent of an activity—a more cautious approach to policy. Who should bear the burden of proof always is a matter of judgment.

In the case of toxic chemicals, the most striking example of this conservative approach is the Delaney Clause, which prohibits additions of any carcinogenic substance to food, even if there are compensating benefits, even if the substance is only weakly carcinogenic, and even if only trivial amounts of the substance are present. Moreover, recognizing that it is very difficult to prove that a chemical causes cancer in humans, advocates of this policy assumed that any animal carcinogen is also a human carcinogen, even though there are some that are not. They explicitly stated during congressional deliberations that when regulating food additives it is better to err on the side of caution. Because it is so extreme, however, the Delaney Clause has rarely been applied and probably is no longer realistic. As measurement capabilities have improved, virtually all foods now can be shown to contain at least trace amounts of questionable chemicals, and the continued use of saccharin and nitrites are two of several examples of possibly carcinogenic substances that continue to be added to foods in order to gain substantial benefits.

Current pesticide regulations also mandate caution, including explicit requirements for manufacturers to bear the burden of proof that a pesticide is safe enough. But this cautious approach becomes difficult to apply in practice. First, Congress requires that EPA evaluate a pesticide's risks against its economic benefits. Second, most pesticides now in use were approved before the current regulations took effect. Moreover, EPA has insufficient staff to carefully scrutinize more than a few dozen pesticide chemicals each year, so a strategy of proceeding cautiously has been adopted in principle but it has not been fully implemented in practice.

Policy on the greenhouse effect to date has not been conservative. In this case, the issue is not how extensive to make the protections but whether to take any precautions at all. Combustion of fossil fuels and production of greenhouse gases have proceeded as if there were no threat, and the burden of proof is on those who challenge these risk-producing activities. On balance, this may be appropriate considering the uncertainties about the greenhouse threat, the benefits of using fossil fuels, and the costs of corrective action. But given the conceivable severity of the consequences, current policy may not be cautious enough. There is a strong temptation to discount future costs of the greenhouse threat in comparison to the near-term costs of preventive action, particularly in view of the unattractive set of alternative actions proposed to date.

The United States and a handful of other nations have proceeded more cautiously against the ozone threat. The SST and aerosol fluorocarbons were banned on the basis of scientific theories, even though there was no direct evidence of harm. Some manufacturers protested the action and called attention to the economic costs, but the majority of atmospheric experts and policy makers found the potential harm sufficiently grave to justify considerable caution. No nation pursued this policy to the fullest, however. Fluorocarbon refrigerants, degreasing solvents, and a variety of chlorocarbon and bromocarbon products continue to be used—initially because they were considered more essential than aerosols, subsequently because the magnitude of the risk appeared to decline.

To reiterate, caution is a matter of degree. Even when policy makers proceed conservatively, they inevitably make controversial judgments. And there will always be dissenters, some with carefully reasoned arguments, who believe that more (or less) caution is warranted. We will consider the issue of "How cautious is cautious enough?" in chapter 8.

Strategy 3: Test the risks

Once conservative measures for coping with the potential hazard are taken, the next step is to reduce uncertainties about the hazard's likelihood and magnitude. One way of doing this is by learning from experience (see strategy 4). An alternative approach for reducing uncertainty is to test for or simulate the hazard under controlled conditions. Unfortunately, as we saw in comparing nuclear power with rDNA research, the uncertainties associated with some hazards are more amenable to testing than others. Testability, like caution, is a matter of degree. At one extreme are the ozone and greenhouse problems; there is no way to realistically simulate these global atmospheric phenomena. At the other extreme is rDNA research, where worst-case scenarios could be simulated under well-controlled laboratory conditions. Toxic chemicals and nuclear reactor safety are cases that fall in the intermediate range. Toxicology in the 1980s bears little resemblance to toxicology of the 1940s, and the capacities of this field are even far ahead of what they were just a decade ago. Short-term screening tests for mutagenicity, analysis of chemicals' effects based on their molecular structures, and powerful new techniques for detecting minute quantities of chemicals are among the improvements that have contributed to toxicologists' ability to discern hazards. Nevertheless important limitations remain. Much of the testing is done with animals; we assume that animal reactions to toxic substances closely approximate those of humans, but we cannot be sure. In addition, it is not feasible to fully test all chemicals (at present more than sixty thousand). Only about two thousand chemicals have been tested adequately for carcinogenicity, fewer for other chronic effects such as liver damage. Even new chemicals are not being tested exhaustively, although all are evaluated to some extent.

The limitations on testing in the case of nuclear power are entirely different. To begin with, there is a matter of scale: in order to simulate a serious reactor accident, a very remote area must be used and a large reactor must melt down. If the critics of nuclear power are correct, the results of such testing could be long-lasting and widespread. However, these considerations by themselves might not be sufficient reason to reject a deliberate meltdown as a means of gaining knowledge and reducing uncertainty. The more important problem is whether we would learn enough from a single meltdown to make the risks worthwhile. Since there are many courses a meltdown could follow and only a small number of possibilities that would occur in a single test, the information gained from even several meltdowns probably would be inconclusive.

To confront these difficulties, one tactic has been to simulate aspects of serious accidents under controlled conditions. Throughout the history of reactor development, relatively small-scale tests have been performed. For example, in the early 1950s a series of experiments were run in which water in small experimental reactors was deliberately allowed to boil. At the time it was feared that boiling water would make reactors unstable and difficult to control, but the experiments showed otherwise. Based on these results, the Atomic Energy Commission and the nuclear industry began to design boiling water as well as pressurized water reactors.

A more recent example of ongoing testing was a July 1985 reactor test made at Idaho Falls. A small reactor was deliberately subjected to a loss of coolant with the objective of obtaining a better understanding of the fission products that are released in serious accidents. This objective was achieved, and the test served its purpose.[3] Many other such tests have been conducted, and they have been very useful for narrowing uncertainties about specific aspects of reactor behavior. But such specialized and limited tests cannot eliminate large uncertainties about overall nuclear risks.

Strategy 4: Learn from experience

An alternative to testing is to learn from experience. This is accomplished by monitoring mishaps that occur despite precautions and by taking steps to prevent such mishaps from recurring. The classic trial-and-error strategy for dealing with complex problems is to: (1) establish a policy, (2) observe the effects of that policy, (3) attempt to correct for any undesired effects, (4) observe the new outcome, and (5) make corrections again. Obviously, regulators should not rely entirely on this strategy (as they did initially in toxic chemicals regulation). But once steps have been taken to protect against potential catastrophe, learning from experience via trial and error is appropriate as a supplemental strategy to reduce uncertainty.

The history of nuclear regulation is replete with examples of trial-and-error learning. Many changes in the regulations governing operator training, design of reactor control panels, operation, maintenance, and emergency procedures evolved in response to the lessons learned from the Three Mile Island accident. While TMI is an extreme case, it is by no means an exception. Regulatory changes in response to reactor incidents have been the rule in the history of nuclear regulation—so much so that the nuclear industry and some policy analysts have criticized regulators for overreacting to these incidents. The same pattern of learning from experience emerges in other cases. Relatively stringent safety guidelines were established in the mid-1970s for rDNA research and then were gradually relaxed. This was partially in response to the results of testing but also partially in response to actual experience with rDNA experimentation. Regulators likewise have learned from experience in toxic substances control. For example, the discovery of badly flawed and even fraudulent toxicology testing has led government agencies to conduct routine audits of independent testing laboratories, and the Interagency Testing Committee has learned from experience to recommend individual chemical substances for testing rather than broad categories of substances.

While learning from experience plays a prominent role in the cases discussed, it nevertheless is the least developed and most poorly implemented of the catastrophe-aversion strategies. Learning from experience too often has been a purely reactive strategy—regulators wait for errors to emerge, then make corrections. In a well-designed catastrophe-aversion system, however, regulators would anticipate employing this strategy, and before errors actually emerged, they would structure the regulatory system so that these errors would receive immediate attention for corrective action. On this score, our current efforts to deal with potentially catastrophic technologies are not sufficient. How we might improve the strategy of learning actively from error is discussed further in chapter 8.

Strategy 5: Set priorities

Priority setting is a fifth strategy that works interactively with the strategies of testing and learning from experience. In the cases reviewed in this volume, the possible risks were so numerous and varied that it was impossible to evaluate all of them at once. Regulators had to set priorities for which risks to study, and at any given time, they focused attention on only small subsets of the possible hazards. This strategy provided a framework for testing and monitoring experience.

The most formal and explicit priority-setting strategy has been used in the toxic chemicals case. For existing chemicals, the Interagency Testing Committee explicitly designates the few chemicals each year that are most in need of additional testing. In the process of regulating new chemicals through the premanufacture notification system, whole classes of less dangerous chemicals are exempted from regulation. Attention can thereby be focused on classes of chemicals that pose a greater threat. For all types of chemicals, EPA uses three criteria to help quickly set priorities: production volume, structural similarity to known carcinogens, and exposure patterns. It is unlikely that these criteria will catch every danger. But considering the alternative—being overwhelmed by the number of possible dangers—priority setting is by far the lesser evil.

In the case of rDNA research, initial testing of possible risks focused on worst-case scenarios and on *E. coli* K-12, the most commonly used host organism for rDNA experiments. Decision makers at least implicitly made it a priority to study the gravest potential dangers in the greatest number of experiments.

As is true for learning from experience, there is considerable room for improvement in how regulators of risky technologies set priorities for testing and monitoring. Our analysis of the greenhouse case, for example, demonstrated the need for more formal priority setting to identify the crucial uncertainties.

In the regulation of nuclear power, attention has shifted from one issue to the next in reaction to events rather than as a result of any deliberate priority setting. Among other difficulties, this can result in a preoccupation with less important issues. For example, in a critique of current practices of the Nuclear Regulatory Commission, political scientist Aaron Wildavsky recommends that the NRC establish meaningful priorities by limiting the number of design changes for nuclear plants already in operation or under construction. Rather than forcing all nuclear plants to conform to the state-of-the-art, Wildavsky argues that more effective regulation could be achieved by requiring only those changes "deemed essential to meet performance standards."[4] At present, the

NRC has so many regulations and design changes that the important ones become confused with the less important ones, and monitoring of key performance aspects becomes extraordinarily difficult.

The complete catastrophe-aversion system

These five strategies for coping with the potential for catastrophe jointly compose a complete, integrated system:

1. Protect against the possible hazard; do so conservatively (strategies 1 and 2).

2. Reduce uncertainty; do so through prioritized testing and prioritized monitoring of experience (strategies 3, 4, and 5).

3. As uncertainty is reduced and more is learned about the nature of the risk, revise the original precautions: strengthen them if new risks are discovered or if the risks appear to be worse than initially feared; weaken them if the reverse proves true.

None of the cases in this volume has completely followed this idealized system. The monitoring and regulatory schemes for the particular risk in each case were strong on some points and weak on others. Of the regulatory approaches reviewed here, the one devised for rDNA research most closely approximates a complete catastrophe-aversion system.

As we have mentioned, some critics believe that regulators and the scientific community were too quick to discount the risks associated with rDNA research. But from a purely procedural perspective, the rDNA case comes very close to the ideal for handling technologies that present a potential for catastrophe. In retrospect, since this hazard is more containable and testable than those associated with the other technologies, rDNA research was the easiest problem to deal with. Nevertheless, the rDNA regulatory system provides a model of how society should cope with a high degree of uncertainty about risks combined with the potential for catastrophe.

136   AVERTING CATASTROPHE

Protective action was taken against the potential hazard of rDNA research by prohibiting the most risky experiments, rating all others according to degree of risk, and requiring prevention and containment measures based on the degree of riskiness. Uncertainty was reduced by learning from experience and through a deliberate program of risk assessment, including a number of worst-case scenario experiments. As uncertainty was reduced, the guidelines and prohibitions were gradually and sequentially adjusted.

While the exact mix of strategies appropriate in a given case obviously depends on the nature of the particular problem, the catastrophe-aversion strategy outlined above should be applicable to virtually any risky technology. Even without a clear perception that such a repertoire of strategies was evolving, society has been using these catastrophe-aversion measures. With an increased appreciation of the options, more systematic application of these strategies should be well within reach. Among other advantages, partisans and policy analysts attempting to map regulatory options will have a far more systematic framework within which to operate.

The catastrophe-aversion system formulated here is relatively simple, moreover, so there is a chance that it can be diffused gradually to a wide audience. It has not been our subject here, but the need for better public and media understanding of risky technologies is a widely shared belief among risk professionals.[5] Such understanding would be valuable in itself for easing public anxiety where it is excessive—and for increasing concern about some risks that now are receiving too little emphasis. Such improvements in the perspectives on risk management held by the media and the general public eventually should result in better allocation of governmental concern and risk-abatement expenditures.

Chapter 8 considers ways of improving the application of the catastrophe-aversion system. The remainder of this chapter attempts to distill the implications of our cases for professional thought about decision making under uncertainty and related topics. It is intended especially for social scientists; some readers may wish to skip directly to the concluding chapter, and can do so without losing the thread of the argument.

Implications for Social Science

Could contemporary theories of decision making have predicted what we would find in our five case studies? Not in sufficient detail to be interesting or useful, we believe. Could contemporary scholarship offer a rich set of recommendations about how to improve the strategies available for regulating risky technologies? Again, we find the relevant literature lacking. The cases examined in this volume suggest that the practice of decision making has advanced beyond available theory. What reassessment would enable theory to catch up to practice?

Analytic versus strategic decision making

Scholarship on decision making tends to divide into two approaches: analytic and strategic.[6] Using the analytic approach, a decision maker attempts to maximize the "expected value" of a choice.[7] He or she must make an exhaustive search for alternatives, identify the consequences of each alternative, and predict the likelihood of each of the consequences of each alternative.[8] Unfortunately, these requirements are impossibly demanding for any but the most simple of decision problems. They require precisely the conditions that most decision makers are denied: unambiguous information (to define the problem and analyze alternative solutions); time, money, and control over the environment (to enable the search for alternative solutions and the analysis of consequences); powerful causal models (to aid in analyzing consequences); and a complete, consistent way to order preferences (to estimate the relative value of the various consequences).

As an alternative to the analytic model, Simon, Lindblom, and others have proffered a set of decision theories we refer to as the "strategic approach." These include Simon's model of general problem solving, Lindblom's disjointed incrementalism and partisan mutual adjustment, March and Simon's approach to decision making in formal organizations, March's "garbage can" model, Steinbruner's "cybernetic paradigm," Etzioni's "mixed scanning" perspective, Dror's effort to synthesize the disjointed-incremental and rational models, and other theories.[9] These approaches to decision making differ in their description and prescription of search procedures, modes and means of analysis, decision rules, and preference structures. But all begin with the premise that decision makers face complex problems with uncertain information, inadequate resources, and ambiguous and sometimes conflicting values. All take as their central thesis that decision makers respond to these unhappy conditions by monitoring feedback from their choices and then adjusting those choices accordingly. All of these approaches are elaborate variations on a trial-and-error strategy.

The type of decision making apparent in our cases does not entirely fit either the analytic or the strategic approach but is clearly much closer to the latter. The decision makers in these cases exhibited a more deliberate and evolved form of the strategic model than the literature predicted. While these decision makers did employ certain elements of the analytic approach, it was typically in support of strategy rather than in its stead.

Matching strategy to problem

Our decision makers were most like the strategic and least like the analytic type in their orientation toward learning from error—the sine qua non of the strategic approach. The underlying logic of the catastrophe-aversion system is to allow decision makers to learn, in time and with experience, more about the nature of the hazard and then evolve the necessary responses to it. This requires taking initial precautions, being conservative in the face of uncertain and potentially grave risks, and enhancing these approaches with testing, monitoring experience, and priority setting.

If there is a difference between our cases and the literature on strategic decision making, it is that in our cases there is more orientation toward learning as an explicit and deliberate part of decision making than is implied by existing theory. Lindblom's decision makers, for example, do not need to be aware that they are pursuing a strategy of serial adjustment to error; perhaps they even need to *not* be aware of it. The "intelligence" of democracy is that diverse participants need only be concerned with pursuing their own partisan interests in order for serial adjustments of error (and gradual improvement of policy) to occur. Likewise, Simon's individual decision makers need not know that they are being boundedly rational. The constraints on their actions are determined by factors such as organizational structure, procedures, and training; they never really need to be aware that their calculations, deliberations, and actions are being constrained (in organizationally rational directions).

In contrast, our cases reveal that decision makers can deliberately adjust their strategies. They still rely on learning from error, but because the consequences of error are so much more severe than for ordinary problems, these decision makers cannot afford the luxury of the traditional approach of waiting for errors to emerge before undertaking corrective action. Decision makers implicitly, and sometimes explicitly, attempt to create conditions that would lead to learning from error—conditions that would protect them from the worst consequences of error while at the same time allowing them to learn from those errors.

Because of the differences in the problems encountered, regulating risky technologies required substantial and deliberate variations in strategy from one technology to the next, and therefore, decision makers deliberately adjusted their strategies in accordance with the nature of the problem. This is best illustrated in the variations we discovered in the first of the five strategies, initial protections against possible hazards: the tactics to regulate toxic substances, nuclear power, rDNA research, and atmospheric threats were all different.

In each of these cases, then, there is a heightened or more advanced form of the strategic model in which the trial-and-error process emerges as a variable under the decision maker's control. The goal is to create a set of conditions that will allow decision makers to proceed through serial adjustment to error while simultaneously protecting society from the potentially harmful consequences of error. Decision makers' tactics vary with the nature of the risk. Decision making thus becomes a partly deliberate process of matching the strategy to the problem.

What role for analysis?

Even though our cases do not reflect the aspirations for rigorous analysis advocated by the analytic approach to decision making, analysis nonetheless plays a prominent role in regulating risky technologies. But the role of analysis is not explained adequately by either analytic or strategic theorists of decision making. We suggest that analysis is most appropriate when it is used *in support of strategy*.

Use of analysis in support of strategy is perhaps best illustrated in the rDNA case. First, measures were taken to protect against the potential hazard, then tests were run to determine whether the most severe of the presumed hazards were real. When these tests proved negative, the protective precautions were relaxed somewhat, and new tests were made on the remaining presumed hazards. Once again the safety precautions were adjusted according to the results of the tests. More tests on still other presumed hazards were made and were followed by further adjustments. The individual tests were not intended to prove rDNA research safe or unsafe, rather they were designed to provide specific data that could be used to narrow critical uncertainties. The accumulated clarifications allowed informed judgments concerning whether to tighten or loosen, at the margins, the tactics that had been deployed in support of an overall regulatory strategy. Analysis was extraordinarily important in this process, but it was integrated with and directed by a set of regulatory strategies. Analysis was not an alternative to strategy.

In the case of nuclear regulation, in contrast, nuclear advocates seemed at times as if they wanted to substitute analysis for a crucial part of the regulatory strategy. During the 1970s after the scaleup in reactor sizes required an emphasis on prevention, some regulators and activists advocated the use of probabilistic risk assessment for calculating absolute levels of reactor safety. But other professionals argued that such risk assessments were not well suited for measuring absolute levels of risk; rather they were useful for identifying weak links in reactor designs, thus indicating where wider margins for error or other tactics were needed to improve relative safety. Such analyses help set priorities for focusing additional attention; but they could not reliably be used to determine the absolute safety of a reactor (that is, how likely an accident would be and how much damage it would cause).[10] In other words, probabilistic risk assessment is an analytic tool to be used in support of strategy, not in place of it. But the NRC had not fully learned this lesson as late as 1985.[11]

Analysis likewise threatens to overwhelm strategy in the greenhouse case. As discussed in chapter 6, attempts to reduce uncertainty about the timing and severity of the problem have been the dominant activity. This may be appropriate given the ambiguities about when climate changes will begin, the marked uncertainty about the effects, and the costs of action. However, the analysis is not being conducted strategically. It suffers from a lack of priority setting. Insufficient attention has been given to identifying and focusing research on the key uncertainties that would be important for policy makers. Moreover, the research focuses too exclusively on atmospheric science and oceanography, with little analysis of options for coping with or avoiding climate changes.

These cases, then, show analysis used in support of strategy, but they also indicate that such use of analysis is not yet widely understood or consistently applied. The regulation of risky technologies is handicapped by efforts to use analysis for inappropriate tasks and by failures to use analysis where it could be extraordinarily helpful.[12]

Other types of problems

Our central concern has been the need to modify the trial-and-error strategy for problems that present a potential for catastrophe. Are risky technology decisions a special case, or are there other types of problems that require modification of traditional decision-making strategies?

There are reasons to suppose that decision makers in other policy areas also face problems that are inappropriate for normal trial and error. The two necessary conditions for trial and error to work well are: the effects of errors must be bearably mild, and intelligible feedback must be available relatively

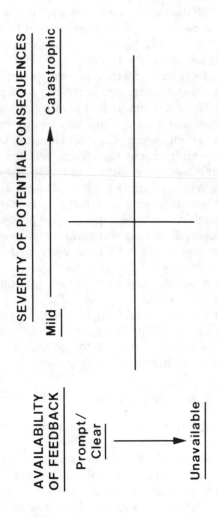

Figure 4. *Variations in the appropriateness of pure trial and error*

promptly after a policy is initiated. Negative consequences of errors obviously can range from relatively mild to catastrophic, while feedback can vary from prompt and clear to unavailable. So these two conditions are in fact variables, or dimensions, and can be used to form a simple matrix (see Figure 4), which illustrates variations in the need to match decision strategy with problem type.

Normal trial and error is most appropriate when consequences of error are relatively bearable and feedback is relatively forthcoming (see the upper left hand quadrant of the figure). The traditional literature on strategic decision making implies that most problems are of this type. Normal budgeting, some economic policy, and noncrisis foreign policy are examples where policy making is a matter of attending to certain critical variables (such as money supply), monitoring the effects of policy on those variables (such as whether the money supply is exceeding targeted levels), and adjusting policy accordingly. The theories that direct such adjustments may vary substantially (as in the case of monetarists versus Keynesians), but the underlying process remains very much one of serial adjustment to relatively forthcoming feedback about relatively bearable errors.

But these conditions do not always hold even for ordinary domestic policy. Sometimes the consequences can become relatively severe, such as when the economy goes into a serious recession. Sometimes feedback is unclear or decision makers cannot afford to wait for it. Under such conditions, the appropriateness of normal trial and error is open to question. Exactly where this point is reached on our two dimensions is hazy, and the complete range of potential strategies for modifying trial and error is by no means apparent. That, however, is precisely our point: neither the empirical nor the normative decision-making literature provides much guidance about conditions under which trial-and-error strategies should be adjusted, how commonly such adjustments are required, or what the adjustments should be.[13]

The risky technologies we have studied obviously fall outside the upper left hand quadrant of the matrix since they all have a potential for catastrophe. In addition, for several technologies the feedback about errors tends to be delayed. The strategies we discovered addressed both these conditions, although our analysis emphasized severity of errors more than delayed feedback. A different mix of strategies presumably would be appropriate for problems with different characteristics. While we cannot explore this possibility in depth here, it is useful to consider the following types of decision problems that have different feedback and consequence patterns.

Delayed feedback.   In the lower half of the matrix, one type of obstacle occurs when there is a time lag between policy and consequence. Obviously, serial adjustment to error is inappropriate if errors in policy do not become apparent for long periods of time. The most extreme example of such a problem is nuclear waste disposal where some consequences might not be apparent for hundreds or even thousands of years.

Even time lags of only a few years can sometimes block the normal process of serial adjustment to error. The Manhattan Project undertaken during World War II is a classic example. Speed in developing the bomb was considered essential during the project, partly because policy makers feared that the Germans were making rapid progress in developing their own bomb. The key element in developing the bomb was the production of enriched uranium. The problem was that each of the alternative approaches for enriching uranium was fraught with uncertainties. Because of the emphasis on speed, decision makers could not afford to rely on ordinary trial and error; they did not have the time to try one approach, wait for feedback, and then change approaches. Their response to this dilemma was to modify the basic strategy: they pursued several alternative approaches simultaneously and then made adjustments as feedback on each emerged.

This simultaneous trials strategy was employed again in the early 1950s in the development of the nuclear submarine and again in the late 1950s in the development of nuclear power reactors. This strategy is now common in industrial research and development when decision makers cannot afford to wait for feedback. Some similar adjustment in decision strategy must be made whenever delayed feedback is expected to interfere with normal trial and error.

Unclear feedback.   Feedback also can be problematic when the causal links between trial and error are obscure or complex. Imagine that a police department changes its crime fighting tactics—for instance, it puts more officers on beats in the subways or more patrol cars in high crime districts. Subsequently, crime rates decline. Should we infer from this feedback that the change in tactics succeeded? Possibly, but the feedback could result from other changes. Even if we set aside questions about the reliability of crime statistics, the decline in crime rate could be due to changes in the economy, other social programs, or even the weather. Alternatively, suppose the crime rate increased. The new tactics might be judged a failure when in fact the changes might actually have had a positive effect that was offset by countervailing changes in other variables. This would be enough of a problem, but if this phenomenon was not recognized, spurious conclusions could be drawn. If decision makers mistakenly learn from experience about a tactic that reduces crime, they may apply the same tactic to different situations only to find to their surprise that it does not work.[14]

How common are problems in which the causal links between trial and error are unclear? LaPorte et al. suggest that many social problems that are treated in relative isolation from one another are, in fact, definitely interconnected. They might be thought of as "semi-lattices," rather than the nearly decomposed or independent systems often assumed by decision theorists.[15] In the social policy arena—poverty, education, crime—we suspect that unclear causal links may be more the rule than the exception, but there has not been enough analysis of this matter to reach firm conclusions.[16] Our point is that normal trial and error implies relatively straightforward causal links between policy choices and subsequent feedback, and on many occasions these links are unclear.

Is there a strategy for modifying normal trial and error that can be used for these cases? The answer is unclear. One approach has been, in Wildavsky's terms, a "strategic retreat from objectives."[17] Rather than continue to try to solve social problems made difficult by these extensive interconnections, an alternative is to pursue more modest objectives. In the criminal justice arena, for instance, some professionals have retreated from the goal of rehabilitating criminals; the revised objective is merely to take the offender off the streets for a while and make it clear that crime results in punishment.

While strategic retreat is a practical response, it is, in effect, an admission of failure. Since multiply-interconnected problems cannot be solved, we retreat to problems that are more amenable to solution. Is there an alternative to admitting failure when cause and effect are too confused for normal trial and error? Since the problem is that extraneous variables intervene in the cause-effect sequence, the solution is to control these variables. One approach is through so-called quasi-experiments that ordinarily entail a strategically selected pilot program or multiple pilot programs. Just as scientific experiments represent a form of very tightly controlled and monitored trial and error, so pilot programs represent trial and error under quasi-controlled conditions.

Unfortunately, the history of quasi-experimentation has been fraught with political obstacles.[18] Even when such obstacles are overcome, as in the Income Maintenance experiments of the 1970s, the results of a pilot program may be ambiguous. Despite these limitations, quasi-experimentation appears to be the only sensible strategic response (other than strategic retreat) to unclear causal links between trial and error.

Problematic feedback and severe consequences. This brings us to the worst of both worlds, where decision makers face problems on which feedback is unavailable and the potential consequences of error are catastrophic. The archetypal example of this situation is crisis decision making. In this type of decision making, information is very scarce, time very short, and the margin for error very narrow.[19] We do not know much about what kinds of decision strategies are appropriate under these conditions. Trial and error is obviously inappropriate; decision makers cannot afford to err, and they do not have the time to wait for feedback.

Thus, the temptation in such cases is to fall back on the analytic approach: if decision makers cannot rely on serial adjustment to error, then they must be as rigorously analytic as possible—identifying objectives, canvasing alternatives, and reviewing information about the possible consequences. Janis and Mann's study of decision making under stress comes close to this prescription.[20] The problem with the analysis-dependent approach is that it assumes the very conditions that decision makers do not have. In crisis decision making, objectives are often ambiguous, alternatives severely constrained, and information about consequences little more than guesswork. However, if decision makers in crises cannot rely on analysis and cannot proceed by trial and error, how should they proceed? This is the dilemma.

There is at least one arena in which strategies have evolved for coping with crisis decision making—pilot and air traffic controller training. An air emergency has all the elements of decision making under crisis: very little time to act, few alternatives, and virtually no margin for error. Pilots and controllers are trained for such crises through simulation exercises. The nuclear industry now is beginning to employ the same techniques for training nuclear power plant operators. These operators will learn how to act in emergencies through simulated trial and error. War games and simulated nuclear attack exercises serve much the same function. Decision makers cannot proceed by trial and error during the real event, so they train for it by learning from simulated events.

While it may be unrealistic to expect a president and his top advisors to subject themselves to simulated crises, perhaps their immediate subordinates should regularly prepare for future crises through simulation exercises and reviews of past crises. If this training was done properly (and this would be no small task), it would help decision makers to identify weak links, likely trouble spots, useful delay tactics, and fallback positions. These skills could prove invaluable in a real crisis.

Conclusion

The combined categories of problem types discussed here are depicted in Figure 5. While too simplified to be anything but suggestive, this representation suggests three conclusions.[21] First, it seems possible to analyze the character of problems; a more in-depth study of problems would need to

Figure 5.   Types of decision problems

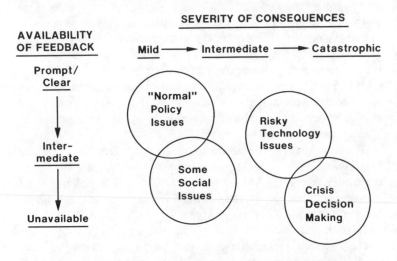

include more dimensions than just consequences and feedback patterns, and it would need to focus on particular problems rather than the combined categories we show.[22] Second, as we evaluated one type of problem after another, we observed that different decision-making strategies emerged; much more investigation is necessary to uncover and specify the complete repertoire of strategies and to link them empirically and normatively with various problem types.

Third, although even sketchier, Figure 5 suggests a way of thinking about the strategies discovered in this volume and of responding more generally to problems that fall outside the upper left quadrant of the matrix. The impulse is to abandon trial and error and to pursue a more analytic approach to such problems. (Technology assessment and risk-benefit analysis are prime examples.) But, as stated, analysis when pursued in isolation from strategy is inappropriate because it requires the very conditions that decision makers do not have.

Instead of abandoning trial and error, the more appropriate course is to artificially create conditions that make serial adjustments possible. In effect, this means restructuring the problem so that it can be handled more like a normal policy issue. If the potential consequences of error are severe, steps should be taken to protect against these consequences, and then decision makers should proceed by trial and error. If the causal links are unclear, steps should be taken to control the intervening variables, and decision makers should then proceed by trial and error. If time lag between trial and error is too long, decision makers should implement several alternatives simultaneously and then proceed by trial and error. In short, if the decision problem is inappropriate for trial and error, decision makers should create conditions that make it more appropriate.

In general, our analysis suggests the need for social scientists to pay more attention to variations in the nature of social problems, to variations in the nature of decision strategies, and to ways of matching strategies to problems.

8

Can We Do Better?

We have already noted that the United States has a better system for diagnosing and averting catastrophes from risky technologies than we had anticipated at the outset of our research. We do not, however, want to overstate this point: it is not a stamp of approval for the overall management of risky technology in the United States. We have been analyzing the possibility of severe physical risks to very large numbers of humans. All we are saying is that there is a good chance in areas of civilian technology that *catastrophes* will be prevented—even in new problem areas where society is not presently expecting trouble. Although it readily could be improved, a monitoring system is in place; and although they could be used better, a repertoire of sensible strategies has been developed to diagnose and prevent potential catastrophes.

We conclude our analysis by examining some of the remaining problems in the management of risky technologies, and by formulating options for improved application of the catastrophe-aversion system.

How Safe Is Safe Enough?

As regulators have developed strategies for coping with potential catastrophes, these very strategies have created a new and sometimes more perplexing problem: when is the catastrophe-aversion system good enough? The question arises because the strategies can be implemented in any number of ways, from very rigorously to very loosely. The second strategy (proceed cautiously), clearly illustrates the problem: How cautious is cautiously? How cautious should be the implementation of initial precautions: very rigorous (early rDNA), moderate (U.S. fluorocarbons), or mild (scrutiny of new chemicals)? No matter how strictly catastrophe-aversion strategies have been applied, they can always be applied even more rigorously—even to the point of an outright ban. The problem would be easily resolved were it not for the fact that the precautions are costly, and each degree of rigor brings additional costs.

Among the cases reviewed here, the problem of weighing the benefits of additional safeguards against the costs is most apparent in the case of nuclear power, and, indeed, is a central element in contemporary nuclear policy debates. Since containment cannot be guaranteed, emphasis is placed on preventing malfunctions and mistakes from triggering serious mishaps. Since prevention requires that all serious possibilities be taken into account, there always seems to be one more set of precautions—and expenses—that perhaps ought to be undertaken. The increase in precautions (and expenses) brings with it the issue of whether additional precautions are worth the cost. Increasingly, new questions are raised: When have we gone far enough in attempting to avoid potential catastrophe? When are reactors safe enough?

The same problem arises, to varying degrees, in our other cases. For toxic chemicals, is it reasonable to focus regulatory concern on the fifty most potentially hazardous substances? Why not twenty, or one hundred, or even five hundred? How many different types of tests should be required, conducted in how many species of laboratory animals? And how dangerous should a chemical be in order to restrict or prohibit its use? The Delaney amendment specifies a zero tolerance for any food additive that causes cancer in animals. But this requirement clearly is too cautious.[1] As toxicologists become able to detect chemicals at the parts per billion or trillion level, virtually all foods will be found to contain traces of something objectionable. The problem thus is similar to the one faced by nuclear regulators when they recognized that containment no longer could be guaranteed in large reactors. In both cases, the zero risk option—no risk of radiation exposures, no trace of a toxic compound—becomes impossible to achieve. Some risk is unavoidable, so the issue is then how much risk is acceptable.

For the greenhouse effect, the same question arises in a somewhat different form. It is not "How far should we go in reducing the risks?" but "How far should we reduce the uncertainties before beginning to reduce the risks?" A potential for catastrophic changes in climate due to greenhouse gases is undeniable, but there remain major uncertainties about the timing and magnitude of the risks as well as the costs associated with the regulatory options. At what point does the likelihood of catastrophe outweigh the costs of action? Possibly this point has not yet been reached, for most scientists and policy makers are still waiting for clarification of the greenhouse threat before deciding whether action is necessary. But this stance rests as much on judgment as on science.

If there is a difference between the greenhouse problem and the nuclear power and toxic substances cases, it is that the nondecision on the greenhouse effect has not been subject to as much controversy. Nevertheless, the potential for yet another open-ended, contentious debate is present, as illustrated by the simultaneous (though coincidental) release in late 1983 of two reports on the greenhouse effect. A National Academy of Sciences report concluded that any responses to the threat should await a reduction in the uncertainties. An EPA report—quickly disavowed by the Reagan administration—concluded the reverse: uncertainties notwithstanding, action should be taken soon. The issue, while not yet a full-blown controversy, looms ahead: how uncertain is uncertain enough?

Another way to put this is, "How much safety should we purchase?" Because people disagree about how much they are willing to spend to reduce risks to health and to the environment, political battles and compromises over safety expenditures are inevitable. This topic is inherently controversial, so it is no surprise that there are long-running, fiercely contested debates. When we consider not just the potential for catastrophe and strategies for avoiding it but also the issue of how stringently to employ those strategies to achieve a sensible balance of costs and benefits, the task facing regulators becomes much more demanding. Whereas regulators seem to be learning to handle the catastrophe-aversion problem, they are having a much harder time with the "How safe?" question.

Setting a safety goal

In the early 1980s, the Nuclear Regulatory Commission made an explicit attempt to resolve the "How safe?" question for nuclear power plants. We review that attempt here to illustrate the nature of the problem and the reasons that it has proven so difficult to resolve. The lessons that can be drawn from this example apply to most risky technologies.

The notion of explicitly addressing the "How safe?" issue emerged well before Three Mile Island, but the accident provided a strong impetus. Several post-accident analyses recommended that the NRC explicitly identify a safety goal—a level of risk at which reactors would be safe enough. Establishing such a goal, advocates believed, would end the interminable debates over whether reactors should be made safer. What quickly became apparent, however, was that establishing a stopping point was far easier to recommend than to achieve. To establish a safety goal, regulators would have to resolve two complex and politically sensitive issues. First, what is an acceptable risk of death and injury? And second, how should regulators determine whether reactors actually pose such an acceptably low risk?

Identifying an acceptable level of risk. A commonly proposed solution to the first problem is to make the acceptable level of risk for nuclear reactors comparable to the risks associated with other technologies.[2] If society has accommodated these other technologies, the argument goes, it is reasonable to assume that society accepts the associated risks.

This approach has proven to be problematic. To begin with, an already accepted technology that bears comparison with nuclear energy is yet to be found. To illustrate this problem, consider the risks of driving an automobile. One can drive a large car or a small one; one can drive cautiously or recklessly, soberly or drunkenly, with seatbelts or without. In contrast, the risks of nuclear power are not as much within the individual's control; the only option an individual has is to move farther away from a reactor. The nature of the hazard associated with these two technologies differs also. Automobiles produce many fatalities through numerous independent events; a serious reactor accident might provide many fatalities from a single event. So does it make sense to compare automobiles with nuclear reactors? Some say "yes"—a death is a death. Others say "no"—high-probability, low-consequence risks that are partially subject to individual control are fundamentally different from low-probability, high-consequence risks over which the individual has no control.

A possible way to overcome this difficulty is to compare the risks from other sources of electricity with those from nuclear power. But this leads to a new problem: how to measure those risks. The hazards of coal are well known—air pollution, acid rain, and possible overheating of the earth's atmosphere—but the level of risk is uncertain.[3] Also in dispute is the range of risks that should be included in such a comparison. Should the risks of mining and transportation be included? What about the risks of waste disposal and sabotage? If the risks of nuclear power are compared to burning oil, what about the risks of a cutoff of oil from the Mideast or the chances of being involved in a war in the Mideast?

Using this comparative approach to define an acceptable level of risk for nuclear power also poses other problems. It assumes that society, after reasoned evaluation, actually has accepted the risks associated with these technologies. Judging from the controversies surrounding air pollution, acid rain, the greenhouse effect, and the health and safety of miners, millions of people do not accept the levels of risk currently posed by coal burning. Moreover, in cases where people seem to accept high risks for an activity that easily could be made significantly safer (such as driving a car), the implicit rejection of precautions that lower risks might not be rational. (Indeed, it is hard to see how the refusal to fasten seat belts can be anything but irrational.) Should the irrational standards that society applies to driving or other unnecessarily risky activities also be applied to nuclear power?

In spite of these problems, the NRC proposed a safety goal in February 1982, after about a year and a half of deliberations. Reactors would be considered safe enough when, among other requirements:

1. The risk to the population near the reactor of being killed in a reactor accident should not exceed 0.1 percent of the risk of being killed in any kind of an accident; and

2. The risk to the population living within fifty miles of the plant of eventually dying from cancer as a result of a reactor accident should not exceed 0.1 percent of the risk of dying from any other causes.[4]

When first proposed, the second of these goals set off a flurry of controversy because 0.1 percent of the cancer rate for a fifty-mile radius would amount to an average of three cancer fatalities per reactor per year. This would be a total of 13,500 deaths over the next thirty years in an industry comprised of 150 reactors—a figure critics argued was too high. The NRC could have responded to this criticism by revising the second goal, but this would have triggered criticism from proponents of nuclear power, who would have argued that the goal was too strict compared with other risks that society accepts. Thus, both parts of the safety goal have remained as originally drafted.

Verifying that the safety goal has been met

If, despite the difficulties, an acceptable level of risk could be agreed on by a majority of policy makers, regulators then would have to determine whether the goal actually has been met. To evaluate this, regulators must know the level of safety achieved by the various safety strategies: they must have the right facts. For nuclear regulators, such a task is even more difficult than identifying an acceptable risk level. The NRC recognized this, and announced that because of "the sizeable uncertainties . . . and gaps in the data base" regarding actual safety levels, the two goals would serve as "aiming points or numerical benchmarks," not as stopping points.[5]

As an illustration of factual uncertainties, consider the first NRC goal concerning the risks of being promptly killed by a reactor accident. Five people in ten thousand are killed by some kind of an accident each year. For a reactor with two hundred people living within a mile, the NRC's goal implies that the annual probability of an accident killing one person should be no more than one in ten thousand.[6] The probability (per reactor per year) of accidents in which ten people are killed should be no more than one in 100 thousand, for one hundred deaths no more likely than one in a million, and so on.

These probabilities are miniscule; they are reassuring because they suggest that the NRC expects serious accidents to be extremely rare. But precisely because the probabilities are so small, it would take hundreds of years for an industry of one hundred reactors to accumulate enough experience to show that reactors satisfy the safety goal. Unless actual probabilities are much higher than those deemed acceptable, experience cannot help in determining whether the risks associated with reactors are as low as stipulated by the safety goal.

The only alternative to learning from experience for determining whether the actual probability of reactor accidents satisfies the safety goal is to use analytic techniques such as fault tree analysis; this, in fact, is how advocates of the safety goal propose to proceed. In fault tree analysis, the analyst attempts to identify all the possible sequences of errors and malfunctions that could lead to serious accidents. For each sequence, the probabilities of each of the errors and malfunctions must be estimated, and from these individual probabilities a probability estimate for the entire sequence is derived. Assuming that the various sequences of events are independent, the analyst then totals the probabilities of each of the sequences. This sum represents the probability estimate of a serious accident.

The key to this form of analysis is that the analyst does not attempt to estimate the probability of a serious accident directly. Because such events have never occurred, there is no data upon which to base an estimate. Instead, the analyst focuses on the sequence of events that would lead to the accident. Unlike the accident itself, the individual events in each of the sequences are relatively common—not only in reactors, but also in a variety of industrial enterprises. For example, the nuclear industry has decades of experience with control rod mechanisms (which control the rate of chain reaction in the reactor), so it is possible to develop fairly reliable estimates of the likelihood that the mechanisms will fail. Similarly, from experience with the nuclear and other industries, it is possible to estimate the probability of power failures, pipe failures, pump failures, and so on.

Unfortunately, fault tree analysis is subject to the same uncertainties that have plagued nuclear regulators since the mid-1960s. What if the analysis fails to identify all the possible sequences of malfunctions that could lead to a serious accident? What if safety systems presumed to be independent actually are vulnerable to common faults? What if the probabilities of inherently uncertain problems, such as operator errors and terrorist attacks, have been underestimated? The regulator must thus confront yet another dilemma: the only practical method for determining the actual probability of reactor accidents is to use analytic techniques, but such techniques are subject to considerable uncertainties. At best, analysis can result in estimates of probabilities. The only way to verify these estimates is through experience, but experience, because of the very low probabilities, is of little help.

Determining whether reactors satisfy a safety goal is further complicated by the fact that the consequences of core melts are uncertain. One of the effects of the mid-1960s shift to a prevention philosophy was that all research about the behavior of core melts halted. The argument was that since core melts were to be prevented, there was no need to study them. As a result, little is now known about the consequences of serious mishaps with the core. Among many other unknowns, it is not clear what portion of the radioactive fission products would actually escape from the reactor in a core melt.[7] It is also not known what would happen to the core if it melted entirely. Its heat might dissipate on the containment floor and the core solidify there instead of melting through. If the molten core came in contact with water accumulated on the containment floor, would it set off a steam explosion? If so, would it be powerful enough to rupture containment?

These and many other aspects of meltdowns are of critical importance in determining the actual risks of reactors, and all of these aspects are uncertain. If the actual risks of reactors are uncertain, then regulators cannot determine with confidence whether the risks associated with reactors are acceptable. They might agree on the levels of risk that would be acceptable, but because of the uncertain probabilities and consequences of reactor accidents, regulators do not know whether the actual risks are as low as required.

In general, most of the proponents of a safety goal failed to appreciate the significance of existing factual uncertainties. They urged the NRC to establish a goal, and (although this step was controversial) the NRC did so. Yet the goal had no impact on the nuclear regulatory process, which currently remains as open-ended and contentious as ever. A safety goal is of little value unless partisans in a dispute can recognize when the goal has been achieved. Ironically, such recognition is prevented by the very uncertainties that made the regulatory process open-ended and led to the demand for a safety goal.

Discussion

Establishing safety goals is the epitome of the analytic approach to risk analysis that dominates professional thinking. Various forms of risk-benefit analysis and cost-benefit analysis are often presented by risk professionals as ways to settle disagreements.[8] To be workable, however, all such analytic methods must confront the same two obstacles that the NRC faced in setting the safety goal: value uncertainties ("And how much for your grandmother?")[9] and factual uncertainties. No analytic methods surmount these obstacles.

With toxic chemicals, for example, regulators are confronted with essentially the same two questions as they are in the nuclear controversy. First, how large a risk of cancer is acceptable? Is it one in one thousand, one in ten thousand, one in a million? And then there is the factual uncertainty that arises with attempts to establish the actual level of risk. Chemical testing typically is performed with animals. Are the responses in animals comparable to responses in humans? Are the dosage rates comparable? Is it even possible to define the human population at risk? As with nuclear power, these questions are answered largely with assumptions, and to a considerable extent, the assumptions are untestable in practice.

For example, the pesticide EDB produces cancer in animals exposed to high dosage levels. We make the conservative assumption that it will do so in humans as well, but we may never be able to test this assumption. Obviously, we would not want to use humans as test subjects, so the only alternative is to use epidemiological evidence—to study exposed populations. Such study is problematic, however, since the population that might be tested for low exposures to EDB might simultaneously have been exposed to so many other possible sources of cancer that it becomes impossible to link cause and effect. We can identify the presence of EDB and, in some cases, levels of exposure to it, but in practice we are not able to establish a close relationship to the possible effects.

It becomes apparent, on reflection, that there is something inappropriate about applying an analytic solution to risk disputes. Even putting aside all the practical difficulties of verifying when a safety goal has actually been achieved, the idea that conflicts of value can be reduced to a formula is at odds with the way that real people and real societies actually function. Of course, as discussed, society does in a certain sense, implicitly accept various levels of risk from technologies now in use. But most people find it morally offensive to plan explicitly for the number of deaths and injuries that will be acceptable. Thus, it is not surprising that there is reluctance to directly confront the "How safe?" problem, even if it is "rational" to do so.

Moreover, while governments frequently deal with value-charged social issues (such as abortion), these issues rarely are quickly resolved. Instead, elements of the issue will repeatedly show up on governmental agendas over decades, producing compromises that gradually evolve with changing social mores.

Analytic strategies rarely, if ever, affect these outcomes, and there is little reason to expect that the value side of risk disputes will depart from this pattern. To be workable, theories of risk management must be compatible with how society's value decisions actually are made.

In principle, establishing a safety target is a perfectly rational approach to improving the catastrophe-aversion system. In practice, it requires that touchy and politically charged value judgments be backed up by factual judgments that are difficult or impossible to verify. So analysis inevitably falls short, as illustrated in the cases studied. While analysis often can be useful as an adjunct, it rarely is a substitute for judgment and strategy.

A Strategic Approach to Improved Risk Management

To improve the efficiency and effectiveness of the catastrophe-aversion system, we must adopt a more strategic approach. We see four promising steps.

1. Attack egregious risks—those clearly worse than others even after allowing for uncertainties;
2. Seek and employ alternatives that transcend or circumvent risks;
3. Develop carefully prioritized research strategies to reduce key uncertainties;
4. Be actively prepared to learn from error, rather than naively expecting to fully analyze risks in advance or passively waiting for feedback to emerge.

Attack egregious risks

Because resources always are limited, society is forced to set priorities. Dollars spent to avert catastrophes are not available for social services. Money spent to avert one type of catastrophe is not available for averting other types. Priority setting can be done in a relatively systematic manner, or it can be done haphazardly. Priorities are now set haphazardly; we are grossly inconsistent in our attempts to reduce various kinds of risks. For example, chemical wastes are many times greater in volume than radioactive wastes, and some are actually longer lived. Yet they tend to be buried in insecure landfills near the surface of the earth, rather than in the deep geological repositories being designed for radioactive wastes; and EPA regulations require that hazardous wastes be contained for only thirty years, compared with ten thousand years for radioactive wastes. And why do we worry about some exposures to radioactivity and not about others? In the mid-1970s, Swedish scientists examining newer housing found high levels of radon from concrete containing alum shale, high in radium. Researchers subsequently have found alarming levels of indoor radon in many parts of the United States; even average homes expose occupants to a cancer risk greater than that posed by most dangerous chemicals. Remedial steps to reduce radon risks are available, but regulation had not been initiated by 1986.[10]

This inconsistency in our approach to risks is by no means an exception, as we can see from the following data:[11]

Safety Measure	Estimated Cost per Life Saved
Cancer screening programs	$10,000+
Mobile cardiac emergency units	$30,000
Smoke protectors	$50,000+
Seat belts	$80,000
Emergency core cooling system	$100,000
Scrubbers to remove sulfur dioxide from coal-fired power plants	$100,000+
Auto safety improvements, 1966–1970	$130,000
Highway safety programs	$140,000
Kidney dialysis treatment units	$200,000
Automobile air bags	$320,000

Proposed upholstered furniture flammability standard	$500,000
Proposed EPA drinking water regulations	$2.5 million
Reactor containment building	$4 million
EPA vinyl chloride regulations	$4 million
OSHA coke fume regulations	$4.5 million
On-site radioactive waste treatment system for nuclear power plants	$10 million
OSHA benzene regulations	$300 million
Hydrogen recombiners for nuclear reactors	$3 billion

This study shows that certain design changes in nuclear reactors would cost as much as $3 billion per life saved, whereas additional highway safety could be achieved for as little as $140,000 per life. Other analyses have resulted in somewhat different estimates, but it is clear that there is a vast discrepancy concerning funds spent to save lives from various threats.

Focusing political attention on the overall costs of averting risks would help balance such gross discrepancies. One course would be to establish a government agency or congressional committee with authority to set priorities for risk reduction. A more realistic option would make total expenditures subject to a unified congressional authorization procedure. Currently, competing proposals for risk abatement do not confront one another. New safety procedures required by the NRC for electric utilities that use nuclear power in no way impinge on the amount spent for highway safety, nor does either of these expenditures influence expenditures for testing and regulation of chemicals. The result is that safety proposals are not compared with each other, so neither government nor the media nor the public is forced to think about comparative risks.

Factual uncertainties prevent precise comparisons among risks, but precise comparisons often are not needed. There are such gross discrepancies in our approaches to different risks that much can be done to reduce these risks without having to confront the intractable uncertainties. Compared to attacking egregious risks that have been relatively unattended, making precise comparisons among risks that already are regulated seems like fine tuning. While it might be nice to make precise comparisons and resolve the "How safe?" debate, doing so is not as important as attacking the egregious risks. Unfortunately, such fine tuning preoccupies professional risk assessors, regulators, and political activists and results in a waste of time and energy.

Transcend or circumvent risks

A second strategic approach would take advantage of risk-reduction opportunities that circumvent troublesome risks. The greenhouse issue provides a good illustration. As discussed in chapter 6, virtually all attention devoted to this problem has focused on carbon dioxide emissions from combustion of fossil fuels. Yet fossil fuels are considered fundamental to contemporary life, and the costs of significant reductions in their use could be severe; so there is widespread reluctance to take any action without a much better understanding of the risks. The net effect is that we wait and debate whether the risk is real enough to warrant action. Until the uncertainties are reduced, there is no rational basis for resolving the debate.

But there may be an alternative. Carbon dioxide is not the only contributor to the greenhouse problem. Other gases, such as nitrous oxide, are also major factors. It is conceivable that emissions of these other gases might be easier to control and might thereby offer an opportunity to at least delay or reduce the magnitude of the greenhouse effect. The 1983 NAS and EPA studies make note of this possibility but do not analyze it in any detail.[12] By early 1986 little sustained attention had been paid to the policy options potentially available for reducing non-CO_2 greenhouse gases.

Similarly, discussions of the options for combating the greenhouse effect have focused on costly restrictions on the use of high carbon fuels, but it may be possible to achieve at least some of the benefits of such restrictions through a much less costly combination of partial solutions. This combination of solutions might include partial reforestation, plus research on crop strains better adapted to dry climates, plus partial restrictions on only the highest carbon fuels.

Another means of circumventing uncertainties about a risk is to develop a method of offsetting the risk. Quite inadvertently, the ozone threat eased when it was found that low-flying airplanes emit chemicals that help produce ozone. Could a similar approach be pursued deliberately for some technological risks? In the greenhouse case, deliberate injection of sulphur dioxide or dust into the atmosphere might result in temporary cooling similar to that achieved naturally by volcanic dust. Deliberate intervention on such a scale might pose more environmental danger than the original problem, but careful analysis of this possibility surely is warranted.

The case of nuclear power provides another possible approach to circumventing risks and uncertainties about risks. Interest is growing in the notion of inherently (or passively) safe reactors—reactors for which there is no credible event or sequence of events that could lead to a meltdown. The reactor concepts now receiving the most attention include small high temperature gas cooled reactors and the PIUS reactor (a light water reactor with the core immersed in a pool of borated water).[13] Preliminary analyses indicate that these reactors are effectively catastrophe proof. Even if the control systems and cooling systems fail, the reactors will still shut themselves down.

Skeptics argue that the concept of inherent safety probably cannot be translated into practice, and that such reactors in any case would not be economical. But in the history of commercial power reactors there has never before been a deliberate attempt to build an inherently safe reactor, and some analysts believe that these new reactors can provide, if not "walk away" safety, at least substantially reduced risks. If this is true, these new reactor concepts provide the opportunity to short circuit much of the "How safe?" debate for nuclear power plants. If it can be shown that such reactors are resistant to core melts in all credible accident scenarios, then many of the open-ended and contentious safety arguments could be avoided. While we do not know whether inherently safe reactors will prove feasible, and while there are other controversial aspects of the nuclear fuel cycle (particularly waste disposal), nonetheless, the possibility that reactors could approach inherent safety is well worth considering. Resistance to this concept apparently is due more to organizational inertia than to sound technical arguments. Thus, in spite of the fact that the concept of inherent safety has been in existence for thirty years, society has been subjected to a bitter and expensive political battle, that a more strategic approach to this topic might have circumvented.

A very different approach to transcending factual uncertainties is to compromise. When policy makers are at an impasse over how safe a technology is or should be, it may at times be possible to reach a solution that does not depend on the resolution of the uncertainties. This strategy is already used, but it is not employed consciously enough or often enough. Because each opportunity for creative compromise necessarily is unique, there can be no standard operating procedure. However, examples of the advantages of compromise abound.

For example, the Natural Resources Defense Council, EPA, and affected industries have reached several judicially mediated agreements that have accomplished most of the limited progress made to date against toxic water pollutants.[14] Another example is the negotiated approach to testing of priority chemicals adopted in 1980 by EPA toward the chemical industry. The possibility of creative compromise was not envisioned by the framers of the Toxic Substances Control Act, but neither was it prohibited. Numerous protracted analysis-based hearings and judicial challenges thereby have been avoided, and judging from the limited results available to date, testing appears to be proceeding fairly rapidly and satisfactorily.

Had compromises and tradeoffs been the basis for setting standards throughout the toxic substances field, many more standards could have been established than actually have been.[15] Then they could have been modified as obvious shortcomings were recognized. Of course, compromise agreements can be very unsatisfying to parties on either side of the issue who believe they know the truth about the risks of a given endeavor. But, by observing past controversies where there was under- or overreaction to possible risks, there is a fair prospect that all parties to future controversies gradually will become more realistic.

Reduce uncertainties: Focused research

A third option for strengthening the catastrophe-aversion system is to create research and development programs focused explicitly on reducing key factual uncertainties. This seems an obvious approach, yet it has not been pursued systematically in any major area of technological risk except for recombinant DNA. Of course, regulatory agencies have research and development (R&D) programs that investigate safety issues, but priorities ordinarily are not well defined and research tends to be ill matched to actual regulatory debates.

The greenhouse case again provides a good illustration, particularly since the uncertainties associated with it are so widely recognized as being at the heart of the debate about whether or not action is required. The NAS report could not have been more explicit about the importance of the uncertainties to the greenhouse debate:

> Given the extent and character of the uncertainty in each segment of the argument—emissions, concentrations, climatic effects, environmental and societal impacts—a balanced program of research, both basic and applied, is called for, with appropriate attention to more significant uncertainties and potentially more serious problems.[16]

Yet as clearly as the report recognizes the importance of the factual uncertainties, it fails to develop a strategy for dealing with them. It merely cites a long list of uncertainties that requires attention. As we discussed in chapter 6, the NRC listed over one hundred recommendations, ranging from economic and energy simulation models for predicting long-term CO_2 emissions, to modeling and data collection on cloudiness, to the effects of climate on agricultural pests.

Certainly answers to all of these questions would be interesting and perhaps useful; but, just as certainly, answers to some of them would be more important than answers to others. What are the truly critical uncertainties? What kinds of information would make the biggest differences in deciding whether or not to take action? As R&D proceeds and information is gained, are there key warning signals for which we should watch? What would be necessary to convince us that we should not wait any longer? Policy makers and policy analysts need a strategy for selectively and intelligently identifying, tracking, and reducing key uncertainties.

A similar problem arises in the case of nuclear power. In principle, nuclear regulators should systematically identify the central remaining safety uncertainties—the issues that will continue to lead to new requirements for regulations. Regulators should then devise a deliberate R&D agenda to address such uncertainties. A prime example is uncertainty about the behavior of the reactor core once it begins to melt. Clearly, this lies at the heart of the entire nuclear debate, since the major threat to the public results from core melts. Yet, as we discussed earlier, virtually no research was performed on core melts in the 1960s and 1970s.

Information and research resulting from the experience of Three Mile Island now have called into question some of the basic assumptions about core melts. For example, if the TMI core had melted entirely, according to the Kemeny Commission it probably would have solidified on the containment floor.[17] Even the nuclear industry had assumed that a melted core would have gone through the floor. Moreover, it appears that there were a variety of ways in which the core melt could have been stopped. Prior to the accident, the common assumption was that core melts could not be stopped once underway. Also overestimated, according to some recent studies, is the amount of radioactive material predicted to escape in a serious reactor accident: prior assumptions may have been ten to one thousand times too pessimistic.[18]

If such revised ideas about reactor accidents were to be widely accepted, they would have a substantial effect on the perceived risks of reactor accidents. But all such analyses are subject to dispute. To the extent feasible, therefore, it clearly makes sense to invest in research and development that will narrow the range of credible dispute—without waiting for the equivalent of a TMI accident. As with the greenhouse effect, what is needed is a systematic review of prevailing uncertainties and an R&D program devised to strategically address them. The uncertainties that make the biggest difference must be identified, those that can be significantly reduced by R&D must be selected, and an R&D program focused on these uncertainties must then be undertaken. In other words, a much better job can be done of using analysis in support of strategy.

Reduce uncertainty: Improve learning from error

As noted previously, learning from error has been an important component of the strategies deployed against risky technologies. But learning from error could be better used as a focused strategy for reducing uncertainties about risk. As such, it would constitute a fourth strategic approach for improving the efficiency and effectiveness of the catastrophe-aversion system.

The nuclear power case again offers a good illustration of the need to prepare actively for learning from error. Suppose that a design flaw is discovered in a reactor built ten years ago for a California utility company. Ideally, the flaw would be reported to the Nuclear Regulatory Commission. The NRC would then devise a correction, identify all other reactors with similar design flaws, and order all of them to institute the correction. In actual operation, the process is far more complicated and the outcome far less assured.

To begin with, in any given year the NRC receives thousands of reports about minor reactor mishaps and flaws. The agency must have a method of sifting this mass of information and identifying the problems that are truly significant. This is by no means a straightforward task, as exemplified by the flaw that triggered the Three Mile Island accident. A similar problem had been identified at the Davis-Besse reactor several years earlier, but the information that was sent to the NRC apparently was obscured by the mass of other data received by the agency. Several studies of the TMI accident noted this unfortunate oversight, and concluded that the NRC and the nuclear industry lacked an adequate mechanism for monitoring feedback. In response, the nuclear industry established an institute for the express purpose of collecting, analyzing, and disseminating information about reactor incidents. This action represents a significant advance in nuclear decision makers' ability to learn from experience.

Even with a well-structured feedback mechanism, there are still other obstacles to learning from experience. One such obstacle arises from the contentious nature of current U.S. regulatory environments, which can actually create disincentives to learning. Given the adversarial nature of the nuclear regulatory environment, many in the nuclear industry believe that they will only hurt themselves if they propose safety improvements in reactor designs. They fear that opponents of nuclear power will use such safety proposals to argue that existing reactors are not safe enough, and that regulators will then force the industry to make the change on existing reactors, not just on new ones. This would add another round of costly retrofits.

Another obstacle to learning from experience can arise from the nature of the industry. For example, the nuclear industry is comprised of several vendors who over the years have sold several different generations of two different types of reactors to several dozen unrelated utility companies. Furthermore, even reactors of the same generation have been partially custom designed to better suit the particular site for which they were intended. This resulting nonuniformity of reactor design is a significant barrier to learning from experience, because lessons learned with one reactor are not readily applicable to others.

The design flaw uncovered at our hypothetical California utility's ten-year-old reactor probably can be generalized to the few reactors of the same generation (unless the flaw was associated with some site-specific variation of the basic design). It is less likely to apply to reactors built by the same vendor but of different generations, much less likely to apply to reactors of the same general type made by other vendors, and extremely unlikely to apply to other reactor types. Furthermore, lessons gained from experience in maintaining and operating reactors are also hard to generalize. Since reactors are owned by independent utilities, the experience of one utility in operating its reactor is not easily communicated to other utilities. In many respects, therefore, each utility must go through an independent learning cycle.

There also are significant barriers to learning about most toxic chemicals. The large number of such chemicals, the vast variety of uses and sites, and the esoteric nature of the feedback make the task of monitoring and learning from experience extraordinarily difficult. Yet the EPA's tight budget and the limited resources of major environmental groups means that routine monitoring will not get the attention that is given to other more pressing needs. What a good system for such monitoring would be is in itself a major research task, but just obtaining reliable information on production volumes, uses, and exposures would be a place to start.

The point, then, is that active preparation is required to promote learning from experience. The institutional arrangements in the regulatory system must be devised from the outset with a deliberate concern for facilitating learning from error. In the nuclear power case, the ideal might be a single reactor vendor, selling a single, standardized type of reactor to a single customer. The French nuclear system comes close to this pattern.[19]

Conclusion

In summary, there are at least four promising avenues for applying risk-reduction strategies more effectively. The first strategy is to make an overall comparison of risks and to focus on those that clearly are disproportionate. The second is to transcend or circumvent risks and uncertainties by employing creative compromise, making technical corrections, and paying attention to easier opportunities for risk reduction. The third strategy is to identify key uncertainties and focus research on them. The fourth is to prepare from the outset to learn from error; partly this requires design of appropriate institutions, but partly it is an attitudinal matter of embracing error as an opportunity to learn. Finally, implicit throughout this study is a fifth avenue for improvement: by better under-

standing the repertoire of strategies available for regulating
risky technologies, those who want to reduce technological
risks should be able to take aim at their task more consciously,
more systematically, and therefore more efficiently.
  Of these, the first strategy probably deserves most attention. Attacking egregious risks offers simultaneously an opportunity to improve safety and to improve cost effectiveness. As
an example, consider the 1984 Bhopal, India, chemical plant
disaster.[20] The accident occurred when:

A poorly trained maintenance worker let a small amount of
water into a chemical storage tank while cleaning a piece of
equipment;

A supervisor delayed action for approximately one hour
after a leak was reported because he did not think it significant and wanted to wait until after a tea break;

Apparently as an economy measure, the cooling unit for the
storage tank had been turned off, which allowed a dangerous chemical reaction to occur much more quickly;

Although gauges indicated a dangerous pressure buildup,
they were ignored because "the equipment frequently mal-
functioned";

When the tank burst and the chemical was released, a water
spray designed to help neutralize the chemical could not do
so because the pumps were too small for the task;

The safety equipment that should have burned off the dangerous gas was out of service for repair and anyway was
designed to accommodate only small leaks;

The spare tank into which the methyl isocyanate (MIC) was
to be pumped in the event of an accident was full, contrary
to Union Carbide requirements;

Workers ran away from the plant in panic instead of trans-
porting nearby residents in the buses parked on the lot for
evacuation purposes;

The tanks were larger than Union Carbide regulations
specified, hence they held more of the dangerous chemical
than anticipated;

The tanks were 75 percent filled, even though Union Carbide regulations specified 50 percent as the desirable level, so that pressure in the tank built more quickly and the overall magnitude of the accident was greater.

The length of this list of errors is reminiscent of the Three Mile Island accident. The difference between the two incidents is that TMI had catastrophe-aversion systems that prevented serious health effects, while at least two thousand died in Bhopal and nearly two hundred thousand were injured. Even though the U.S. chemical industry is largely self-regulated, most domestic plants employ relatively sophisticated safety tactics that use many of the strategies of the catastrophe-aversion system. Still, questions remain about how effectively these strategies have been implemented.[21] For example, a 1985 chemical plant accident in Institute, West Virginia, while minor in its effects, revealed a startling series of "failures in management, operations, and equipment."[22]

The Bhopal and Institute incidents suggest that, relative to other risks, safety issues in chemical manufacturing deserve more governmental attention than they previously have received. In addition to whatever changes are warranted at U.S. chemical plants, special attention should be paid to the process of managing risk at many overseas plants owned by U.S. firms. If the practices at the Bhopal plant were typical, safety strategies abroad are haphazard. While the Bhopal incident has led to a fundamental review of safety procedures in chemical plants worldwide, it should hardly have required a catastrophe to reveal such a vast category of hazard. This oversight demonstrates that some entire categories of risk may not yet be taken into account by the catastrophe-aversion system.

The catastrophe-aversion system likewise was not applied, until recently, to hazardous waste in the United States. State and federal laws made no special provision for toxic waste prior to the 1970s; there were no requirements for initial precautions, or for conservatism in the amounts of waste that were generated. Systematic testing for underground contamination was not required, and waste sites were not monitored for potential problems. It is a tribute to the resilience of the ecosystem that after-the-fact cleanup now in progress has a good chance of keeping damage from past dumping below catastrophic levels. The next step is to find ways of limiting the generation of new wastes. What does all this add up to? In our view, society's standard operating procedure should be as follows:

First, apply each of the catastrophe-aversion strategies in as many areas of risk as possible;

After this has been accomplished, proceed with more detailed inquiry, debate, and action on particular risks.

To pursue detailed debates on a risk for which a catastrophe-aversion system already is operative, continuing to protect against smaller and smaller components of that risk, is likely to be a misallocation of resources until the full range of potential catastrophes from civilian technologies has been guarded against. The "How safe?" questions that have become so much the focus of concern are matters of fine tuning; they may be important in the long run, but they are relatively minor compared to the major risks that still remain unaddressed.

Concluding note

At the outset of this volume we quoted a highly respected social critic, Lewis Mumford, who claimed in 1970 that "The professional bodies that should have been monitoring our technology . . . have been criminally negligent in anticipating or even reporting what has actually been taking place." Mumford also said that technological society is "a purely mechanical system whose processes can neither be retarded nor redirected nor halted, that has no internal mechanism for warning of defects or correcting them."[23] French sociologist Jacques Ellul likewise asserted that the technological

system does not have one of the characteristics generally regarded as essential for a system: feedback. . . . [Therefore] the technological system does not tend to modify itself when it develops nuisances or obstructions. . . . [H]ence it causes the increase of irrationalities.[24]

Reflecting on different experiences several decades earlier, Albert Schweitzer thought he perceived that "Man has lost the capacity to foresee and forestall. He will end by destroying the earth."[25]

Although one of us began this investigation extremely pessimistic and the other was hardly an optimist, we conclude that Mumford, Ellul, Schweitzer, and many others have underestimated the resilience both of society and of the ecosystem. We found a sensible set of tactics for protecting against the potentially catastrophic consequences of errors. We found a complex and increasingly sophisticated process for monitoring and reporting potential errors. And we found that a fair amount of remedial action was taken on the basis of such monitoring (though not always the right kind of action or enough action, in our judgment).

Certainly not everyone would consider averting catastrophe to be a very great accomplishment. Most citizens no doubt believe that an affluent technological society ought to aim for a much greater degree of safety than just averting catastrophes. Many industry executives and engineers as well as taxpayers and consumers also no doubt believe that sufficient safety could be achieved at a lower cost. We agree with both. But wanting risk regulation to be more efficient or more effective is very different from being caught up in an irrational system that is leading to catastrophic destruction. We are glad—and somewhat surprised—to be able to come down on the optimistic side of that distinction.

Finally, what are the implications of the analysis in this volume for environmentally conscious business executives, scientists, journalists, activists, and public officials? Is it a signal for such individuals to relax their efforts? We do not intend that interpretation. The actions taken by concerned groups and individuals are an important component of the catastrophe-aversion system described in these pages. To relax the vigilance of those who monitor errors and seek their correction would be to change the system we have described. Quick reaction, sometimes even overreaction, is a key ingredient in that part of regulating risky technologies that relies on trial and error. So to interpret these results as justifying a reduction of efforts would be a gross misreading of our message.

Instead, we must redirect some of our concern and attention. Environmental groups should examine whether they could contribute more to overall safety by focusing greater attention on egregious risks that have not been brought under the umbrella of the catastrophe-aversion system—instead of focusing primarily on risks that already are partially protected against. The Union of Concerned Scientists, for example, devotes extended attention to analyses of nuclear plant safety but has contributed almost nothing on the dangers of coal combustion, international standards for chemical plants, or toxic waste generation—egregious risks that have not been taken into account by catastrophe-aversion strategies. Regardless of whether contemporary nuclear reactors are safe enough, there is no question that they have been intensively subjected to the restraints of the catastrophe-aversion system. We doubt that much more safety will be produced by further debate of the sort that paralyzed nuclear policy making during the 1970s and 1980s. In general, we believe it is time for a more strategic allocation of the (always limited) resources available for risk reduction.

The main message of this volume, however, has been that the United States has done much better at averting health and safety catastrophes than most people realize, considering the vast scope and magnitude of the threats posed by the inventiveness of science and industry in the twentieth century. Careful examination of the strategies evolved to cope with threats from toxic chemicals, nuclear power, recombinant DNA, ozone depletion, and the greenhouse effect suggests that we have a reasonably reliable system for discovering and analyzing potential catastrophes. And, to date, enough preventive actions have been taken to avoid the worst consequences. How much further improvement will be achieved depends largely on whether those groups and individuals concerned with health and safety can manage to win the political battles necessary to extend and refine the strategies now being used. Because we have a long way to go in the overall process of learning to manage technology wisely, recognizing and appreciating the strengths of our catastrophe-aversion system may give us the inspiration to envision the next steps.

Notes

1. The Potential for Catastrophe

1. Barry Commoner, *The Closing Circle: Nature, Man, and Technology* (New York: Alfred Knopf, 1971), 294–95.
2. Roberto Vacca, *The Coming Dark Age* (Garden City, N.Y.: Doubleday, 1973), 3–4.
3. Theodore Roszak, *Where the Wasteland Ends: Politics and Transcendence in Postindustrial Society* (Garden City, N.Y.: Doubleday, 1972), xix.
4. Lewis Mumford, *The Pentagon of Power* (New York: Harcourt Brace Jovanovich, 1970), 410.
5. See David Braybrooke and Charles E. Lindblom, *A Strategy of Decision* (New York: Free Press, 1963); Richard M. Cyert and James G. March, *A Behavioral Theory of the Firm* (Englewood Cliffs, N.J.: Prentice-Hall, 1958); James G. March and Herbert A. Simon, *Organizations* (New York: Wiley, 1958); and John D. Steinbruner, *The Cybernetic Theory of Decision* (Princeton: Princeton University Press, 1974).
6. For additional views on these special difficulties, see Charles Perrow, *Normal Accidents: Living with High-Risk Technologies* (New York: Basic Books, 1984); and Todd R. LaPorte, "On the Design and Management of Nearly Error-Free Organizational Control Systems," in David L. Sills et al., eds., *Accident at Three Mile Island: The Human Dimensions* (Boulder, Colo.: Westview Press, 1982), 185–200.
7. Donella Meadows, John Richardson, and Gerhart Bruckmann, *Groping in the Dark: The First Decade of Global Modelling* (New York: Wiley, 1982), 15.
8. Baruch Fischoff, Paul Slovic, and Sarah Lichtenstein, "Which

Risks Are Acceptable?," *Environment* 21 (May 1979): 17–20, 32–38; quote from 35.

9. Compare the pessimistic perspective on environmental deterioration in Council on Environmental Quality, *Global 2000 Report to the President of the U.S.: Entering the Twenty-First Century* (New York: Pergamon, 1980) with the optimistic view of Julian Simon, *The Ultimate Resource* (Princeton: Princeton University Press, 1981).

10. For a criticism of AEC policy making, see Steven L. Del Sesto, *Science, Politics, and Controversy: Civilian Nuclear Power, 1946–1976* (Boulder, Colo.: Westview Press, 1981). For a brief overview of common criticisms, see Edward J. Woodhouse, "The Politics of Nuclear Waste Management," in Charles A. Walker et al., eds., *Too Hot to Handle?: Social and Policy Issues in the Management of Radioactive Wastes* (New Haven, Conn.: Yale University Press, 1983), 151–83.

11. President's Commission on the Accident at Three Mile Island, *The Need for Change: The Legacy of TMI* (Washington, D.C.: U.S. Government Printing Office, October 1979), 34. Those closest to the plant received an average dose equivalent to about 10 percent or less of the background radiation to which they are exposed each year. Total cancer deaths from the additional radiation could be as low as zero or as high as ten.

12. See, for example, Laura B. Ackerman, "Humans: Overview of Human Exposures to Dieldrin Residues in the Environment and Current Trends of Residue Levels in Tissue," *Pesticides Monitoring Journal* 14 (September 1980): 64–69.

13. A good, comprehensive review of cancer estimates is Richard Doll and Richard Peto, *The Causes of Cancer: Quantitative Estimates of Avoidable Risks of Cancer in the United States Today* (New York: Oxford University Press, 1981).

14. Some U.S. government publications give figures as high as 38 percent, but such calculations do not stand up under scrutiny: the agencies issuing such statistics stand to gain higher budgets if their estimates are accepted. Samuel S. Epstein's *The Politics of Cancer* (Garden City, N.Y.: Doubleday, 1978) likewise overstates the contribution of industrial chemicals to cancer. For further detail, see Doll and Peto, *The Causes of Cancer,* Appendices C, D, and E.

15. A total of approximately 430,000 people per year died of cancer in the mid-1980s, and the number has been increasing each year owing to population growth. Good statistics on the incidence of cancer are unavailable, but the total effects of chemicals would have to be increased to take into account the percentage of people who are cured of cancer or go into remission and die of some other cause.

2. Toxic Chemicals

1. For an excellent overview of pesticide effects on the environment and other aspects of the early feedback process, see James Whorton, *Before Silent Spring: Pesticides and Public Health in Pre-DDT America* (Princeton: Princeton University Press, 1974).

2. Ibid., 23–25.

3. T. H. Haskins, *Garden and Forest* 4 (1891): 247; quoted in Whorton, *Before Silent Spring*, 24.

4. See Whorton, *Before Silent Spring*, 24–25, 212–17.

5. Rachel Carson, *Silent Spring* (Boston: Houghton Mifflin, 1962).

6. The original studies were E. G. Hunt and A. I. Bischoff, "Inimical Effects on Wildlife of Periodic DDD Applications to Clear Lake," *California Fish and Game* 46 (1960): 91–106; and George J. Wallace, "Insecticides and Birds," *Audubon Magazine* 61 (January–February 1959): 10–12, 35.

7. Carson, *Silent Spring*, 129–52.

8. A. W. A. Brown, "The Progression of Resistance Mechanisms Developed Against Insecticides," in Jack R. Plimmer, ed., *Pesticide Chemistry in the 20th Century* (Washington, D.C.: American Chemical Society, 1977), 21–34.

9. Whorton, *Before Silent Spring*, 133–60.

10. Wayland J. Hayes, Jr., et al., "Storage of DDT and DDE in People with Different Degrees of Exposure to DDT," *AMA Archives of Industrial Health* 18 (1958): 398–406. Frank E. Guthrie, "Pesticides and Humans," in Frank E. Guthrie and Jerome J. Perry, eds., *Introduction to Environmental Toxicology* (New York: American Elsevier, 1980), 299–312.

11. For example, see Wayland J. Hayes, Jr., William E. Hale, and Carl I. Pirkle, "Evidence of Safety of Long Term, High Oral Doses of DDT for Man," *Archives of Environmental Health* 22 (1971): 119–35.

12. For two such efforts, see President's Science Advisory Committee, *Use of Pesticides* (Washington, D.C.: U.S. Government Printing Office, 1963); and Department of Health, Education, and Welfare, *Report of the Secretary's Commission on Pesticides and Their Relationship to Environmental Health* (Washington, D.C.: U.S. Government Printing Office, 1969).

13. Some of the newer pesticides are *more* dangerous to agricultural workers, however. EPA's current pesticide regulatory efforts focus in part on worker safety.

14. Roger D. Johnson, Dennis D. Manske, and David S. Podrebarac, "Pesticide, Metal, and Other Chemical Residues in Adult Total Diet Samples, (XII), August 1975–July 1976," *Pesticides Monitoring Journal* 15 (June 1981): 54–65. Also see F. L. McEwen and G. R. Stephenson, *The Use and Significance of Pesticides in the Environment* (New York: Wiley, 1979), especially 365–78.

15. For example, dieldrin levels declined steadily as the pesticide's use was phased out but then plateaued at about 0.2 ppm in human adipose tissues. It is impossible to determine whether there are health effects from such small amounts. Laura B. Ackerman, "Humans: Overview of Human Exposures to Dieldrin Residues".

16. For further details on early legislation and regulations, see Whorton, *Before Silent Spring,* and Edward J. Woodhouse, "Toxic Chemicals and Technological Society: Decision-Making Strategies When Errors Can Be Catastrophic" (Ph.D. diss., Yale University, 1983).

17. The amendment has been interpreted to allow the FDA to block use of an additive, even though available evidence was merely suggestive of possible harm and was inadequate to judge the additive unsafe. See *Certified Color Manufacturers Association v. Matthews,* 543 F. 2d 284 (D.C. Cir., 1976).

18. Testimony of Dr. Lee A. DuBridge, in U.S. Senate Committee on Commerce, Subcommittee on Energy, Natural Resources, and the Environment, *Effects of 2,4,5-T on Man and the Environment: Hearings, June 17–18, 1970,* 91st Cong., 2d sess., 1970, p. 62.

19. This interpretation was made by a court, on the basis of somewhat vague language in the actual statute. See *Environmental Defense Fund* v. *EPA,* 548 F. 2d 998, 9 ERC 1433 (D.C. Cir., 1977).

20. U.S. Council on Environmental Quality, *Toxic Substances* (Washington, D.C.: U.S. Government Printing Office, 1971).

21. The Chemical Abstracts Service, which is responsible for assigning a unique chemical number to each compound, later estimated the number at three hundred to five hundred new compounds annually, and some estimates placed the percentage of dangerous chemicals as low as 5 percent.

22. Senate report 94-698, reprinted in Ray M. Druley and Girard L. Ordway, *The Toxic Substances Control Act,* rev. ed. (Washington, D.C.: Bureau of National Affairs, 1981), 302.

23. For a comparison of the U.S. and European regulations on new chemicals, see Sam Gusman et al., *Public Policy Toward Chemicals: National and International Issues* (Washington, D.C.: The Conservation Foundation, 1980). TCSA also gave EPA new authority over existing chemicals.

24. *Congressional Quarterly Almanac* (Washington, D.C.: Congressional Quarterly, Inc.) 29 (1973): 674 (emphasis added).

25. *Congressional Quarterly Almanac* (Washington, D.C.: Congressional Quarterly, Inc.) 32 (1976): 123.

26. Druley and Ordway, *The Toxic Substances Control Act,* 303.

27. In marked contrast, regulatory agencies still must prove the danger before they can regulate occupational exposures to toxic chemicals, air and water pollutants, drinking water contaminants, cosmetics, and existing chemicals covered by TSCA.

28. On burdens of proof, see David V. Doniger, "Federal Regulation of Vinyl Chloride: A Short Course in the Law and Policy of Toxic Substances Control," *Ecology Law Quarterly* 7 (1978): 497–677, especially 664–65.

29. Compiled from monthly status reports on premanufacture notification for new chemical substances, *Federal Register,* beginning with "Toxic Substances; Premanufacturing Notices; Monthly Status Report," *Federal Register* 44 (May 15, 1979): 28410.

30. For 1984, however, PMN chemicals actually entering production rose to more than 40 percent.

31. References herein to EPA staff and other participants are based on personal interviews conducted by the authors in Washington and by telephone with approximately a dozen high-ranking staff members from EPA, the Interagency Testing Committee, and relevant interest groups.

32. The staffing and budget figures are from internal Office of Toxic Substances budget memoranda supplied to the authors in personal communications.

33. *Toxic Substances Reporter Update,* 1 (August 7, 1981): 6–7. The exemption was requested only for dyes manufactured in annual quantities of 25,000 pounds or less, and the dye would have to meet safety criteria of the Federal Hazardous Substances Act or the American National Standard Institute.

34. See, for example, Office of Technology Assessment, *The Information Content of Premanufacture Notices* (Washington, D.C.: U.S. Government Printing Office, 1983); and U.S. General Accounting Office, *EPA Implementation of Selected Aspects of the Toxic Substances Control Act* (Washington, D.C.: U.S. General Accounting Office, December 7, 1982).

35. *Toxic Substances Reporter Update,* 1 (August 7, 1981): 6.

36. Toxic Substances Control Act, section 4e.

37. For further details on testing of alkyltins, see "Eleventh Report of the Interagency Testing Committee to the Administrator,"

Federal Register 47 (December 3, 1982): 54626–44 (and sources cited therein).
  38. *NRDC* v. *Costle,* 14 ERC 1858 (D.D.C. 1980).
  39. See U.S. General Accounting Office, *EPA Implementation.*
  40. For the NRDC view, see "Comments of the Natural Resources Defense Council, Inc., on Voluntary Testing Programs for the Alkyl Phthalates and the Chlorinated Paraffins: A Critical Review of Their Legal and Scientific Adequacy Under Section 4 of the Toxic Substances Control Act," EPA Office of Pesticides and Toxic Substances memorandum 40009, October 20, 1981.
  41. On the Significant New Use Rules program, see Edward J. Woodhouse, "External Influences on Productivity: EPA's Implementation of TSCA," *Policy Studies Review* 4 (1985): 497–503.

3. Nuclear Power

  1. Early discussions on nuclear power included: "Reactor Hazards Predictable, Says Teller," *Nucleonics* (November 1953): 80; U.S. Congress Joint Committee on Atomic Energy, *Hearings on Government Indemnity for Private Licensees and AEC Contractors,* 84th Cong., 2d sess., 1956; *Hearings on Governmental Indemnity and Reactor Safety,* 85th Cong., 1st sess., 1957; G. Weil, "Hazards of Nuclear Power Plants," *Science* 121 (1955): 315.
  Major studies in the 1970s included: Nuclear Regulatory Commission, *Reactor Safety Study,* Wash-1400 (Washington, D.C.: U.S. Government Printing Office, 1975); and "Report to the APS by the Study Group on Light Water Reactor Safety," *Reviews of Modern Physics* 47 (1975), suppl. no. 1.
  See chapter 8 for recent stages of the controversy.
  2. Richard G. Hewlett and Francis Duncan, *Atomic Shield, 1947–1952* (University Park: Pennsylvania State University Press, 1969), 196.
  3. AEC Reactor Safeguards Committee (RSC) meetings of June and September 1948; systematized in Edward Teller, "Statement on Danger Area Regulations and on Schenectady Intermediate Reactor," November 17, 1948, AEC Archives, discussed and cited in *Atomic Shield, 1947–52*: 195, 204.
  4. Letter from Walter H. Zinn, director of Argonne National Laboratory, to James B. Fisk, July 23, 1948, AEC Archives, cited in *Atomic Shield, 1947–52*: 196.
  5. Edward Teller, letter to George L. Weil on behalf of the RSC,

September 10, 1948, AEC Archives, cited in *Atomic Shield, 1947–52*: 203.

6. C. P. Russel, *Reactor Safeguards* (New York: MacMillan, 1962), 19.

7. *Atomic Shield, 1947–52*: 186.

8. Russel, *Reactor Safeguards*, 20.

9. Richard G. Hewlett and Francis Duncan, *Nuclear Navy, 1946–1962* (Chicago: University of Chicago Press, 1974), 176.

10. *Atomic Shield, 1947–52*: 188, 203.

11. The designs of the land-based versions for each type of reactor were nearly identical to the seafaring versions. The land-based versions served as trial runs. They provided experience in the construction of such reactors (no comparable reactors previously had been built) and they provided an opportunity to discover any serious flaws in the reactor designs before they were built into the seafaring versions.

12. E. S. Rolph, *Nuclear Power and the Public Safety* (Lexington, Mass.: Lexington Books, 1979), 24.

13. Information on the nuclear submarines is still largely classified. Consequently the following discussion of the two tactics does not include specific examples of their application.

14. H. G. Rickover, in Subcommittee on Energy Research and Production of the Committee on Science and Technology, U.S. House of Representatives," 96th Cong., 1st sess., May 22, 23, 24, 1979, 1042.

15. Ibid.

16. See Joint Committee on Atomic Energy, *Government Indemnity for Private Licensees*, 47 ff.; *Hearings on Indemnity and Reactor Safety*, 86th Cong., 1st sess., 1960, 20 ff.; *Hearings on Licensing and Regulation of Nuclear Reactors, Part 1*, 90th Cong., 1st sess., 1967, 62–63, 308 ff.; C. K. Beck et al., "Reactor Safety, Hazards Evaluation and Inspection," in *Proceedings of the Second U.N. International Conference on the Peaceful Uses of Atomic Energy* (New York: United Nations, 1959), 17 ff.

17. On the emergency systems strategy, see Joint Committee on Atomic Energy, *Licensing and Regulation*, 63.

18. C. K. Beck, "U.S. Reactor Experience and Power Reactor Siting," in *Proceedings of the Third International Conference on the Peaceful Uses of Atomic Energy*, vol. 11 (New York: United Nations, 1965), 355.

19. W. K. Davis and W. B. Cottrell, "Containment and Engineered Safety of Nuclear Power Plants," in *Proceedings of the Third*

International Conference on the Peaceful Uses of Atomic Energy, vol.
13 (New York: United Nations, 1965), 367.

20. Containment systems became increasingly sophisticated with
time. By the early 1960s the shields were supplemented by systems for
reducing postaccident temperatures and pressures in the area within
the shield and for washing and filtering out the radioactive fission
products released into the atmosphere within the shield. (By filtering
the products out of the atmosphere, the small rate of leakage of fission
products through the shield could be further reduced.) See ibid.

21. S. G. Kingsley, "The Licensing of Nuclear Power Reactors in
the United States," *Atomic Energy Law Journal* 7 (1965): 341.

22. See especially David Okrent, *Nuclear Reactor Safety: On the
History of the Regulatory Process* (Madison: University of Wisconsin
Press, 1981), chapter 8.

23. The most likely source of a serious accident in a light water
reactor is a loss of coolant. When the coolant is lost—through a
rupture of one of the main pipes, for example—the chain reaction
ends. That is, the reactor shuts itself down. But although the chain
reaction ends, the core continues to give off heat—not nearly as much
as during the chain reaction, but still a substantial amount. The heat
is generated by the energy released in the radioactive decay of the
fission products that were produced during the chain reaction and
that remain in the reactor core after the chain reaction ends. Nor-
mally, this "decay heat" is removed by the reactor coolant. Without
the coolant, however, it cannot be removed, and if this happens, it
will melt the material in which the fuel is enclosed and eventually the
fuel itself. Once the fuel begins to melt, radioactive fission products
are released from the core. The scale-up to more powerful reactors
was important because of this decay heat problem. The more powerful the reactor, the greater the amount of fission products produced
during operation, and consequently, the greater the amount of decay
heat. The greater the amount of decay heat, the more severe the heat
removal problem in a loss-of-coolant accident.

24. See, for example, Okrent, *Nuclear Reactor Safety,* chapters 8
and 11.

25. Ibid., 112.

26. See, for instance, U.S. Congress, Joint Committee on Atomic
Energy, *Hearings on Nuclear Reactor Safety,* 93rd Cong., 1st sess.,
1973, 34. More generally, see U.S. Congress, Joint Committee on
Atomic Energy, *Hearings on AEC Licensing Procedure and Related
Legislation, Parts I and II,* 92nd Cong., 1st sess., 1971; U.S. Con-

gress, Joint Committee on Atomic Energy, *Hearings on Nuclear Reactor Safety,* 93rd Cong., 1st sess., 1973; U.S. Atomic Energy Commission, *The Safety of Nuclear Power Reactors and Related Facilities,* Wash-1250, draft (Washington, D.C.: U.S. Government Printing Office, 1973).

27. While it placed emphasis on prevention, the AEC did not drop the requirement that reactors be built with containment systems. Since these systems would still withstand at least some core melts and would therefore contain the fission products released in those melts, the AEC continued to require that reactors be built with containment systems.

28. W. B. Cottrell, "The ECCS Rule-Making Hearing," *Atomic Energy Law Journal* 16 (1975): 353.

29. Ibid. Also see U.S. Nuclear Regulatory Commission, *Reactor Safety Study,* Wash-1400 (Washington, D.C.: U.S. Government Printing Office, 1975), Appendix XI, 37.

30. Cottrell, "The ECCS Rule-Making Hearing," 354.

31. In addition to being designed redundantly, the new emergency cooling systems also were designed with wide margins of error. Over the course of the late 1960s and early 1970s, as a result of a series of controversies, these margins were repeatedly expanded. For a partial list of these margins, see AEC, *The Safety of Nuclear Power Reactors and Related Facilities,* 5–9.

32. Quoted in Z. D. Nikodem et al., "Nuclear Power Regulation," in *Energy Policy Study,* vol. 10 (Washington, D.C.: U.S. Department of Energy, May 1980), 159.

33. See ibid. See also W. E. Mooz, *Cost Analysis of Light Water Reactor Power Plants* (Santa Monica, Calif.: Rand, 1978).

34. President's Commission on the Accident at Three Mile Island, *The Need for Change: The Legacy of TMI* (Washington, D.C.: U.S. Government Printing Office, October 1979), 56. See also David Okrent and David Moeller, "Implications for Reactor Safety of the Accident at Three Mile Island, Unit 2," in J. Hollander, M. Simmons, and D. Wood, eds., *Annual Review of Energy,* vol. 6 (Palo Alto, Calif.: Annual Reviews, 1981).

35. Ibid., 56.

36. "Assessment: The Impact and Influence of TMI," *EPRI Journal* 5 (June 1980): 30.

37. R. J. Breen, "Defense-in-Depth Approach to Safety in Light of the Three Mile Island Accident," *Nuclear Safety* 22 (1981): 562.

38. Ibid.

4. Recombinant DNA Research

1. See for example, J. Walsh, "Public Attitude Toward Science Is Yes, but—," *Science* 215 (1982): 270; and Paul Slovic et al., "Facts and Fears: Understanding Perceived Risks," in R. C. Schwing and W. A. Albers, eds., *Societal Risk Assessment,* (New York: Plenum, 1980).

2. U.S. Department of Health, Education, and Welfare, National Institutes of Health, "Recombinant DNA Research Guidelines," *Federal Register,* Part II, July 7, 1976. These guidelines have the power of law only for rDNA research performed with NIH funds. Research performed with private funds and with funds from other federal agencies is not legally bound by the guidelines. Nevertheless, as far as can be determined, all recombinant DNA research in the United States has proceeded in accordance with the guidelines. Federal agencies other than the NIH that fund rDNA research require compliance with the guidelines, and privately funded researchers, primarily in industry, have voluntarily complied.

3. The NIH guidelines classified rDNA experiments into four groups according to the degree of hazard. The proposed facility was to be used for experiments falling in the second most hazardous of the four classes.

4. Clifford Grobstein, *A Double Image of the Double Helix: The Recombinant DNA Controversy* (San Francisco: W. H. Freeman, 1979), 66.

5. William Bennett and Joel Gurin, "Science That Frightens Scientists: The Great Debate Over RDNA," *Atlantic* 239 (February 1977): 43; Liebe Cavalieri, "New Strains of Life or Death," *The New York Times Magazine* (August 22, 1976): 8; "Creating New Forms of Life—Blessing or Curse?" *U.S. News and World Report* 82 (April 11, 1977): 80; John Lear, *Recombinant DNA, The Untold Story* (New York: Crown, 1978); Michael Rogers, *Biohazard* (New York: Knopf, 1977); June Goodfield, *Playing God: Genetic Engineering and the Manipulation of Life* (New York: Random House, 1977).

6. Grobstein, *A Double Image,* 75.

7. Authors' interviews with congressional staff, fall 1981.

8. For related discussions, see A. Mazur, "Disputes Between Experts," *Minerva,* 11 (April 1973): 243–62; and Dorothy Nelkin, "The Role of Experts in a Nuclear Siting Controversy," *The Bulletin of the Atomic Scientists* 30 (November 1974): 29–36.

9. Compare U.S. Nuclear Regulatory Commission, *Reactor Safety Study,* Wash-1400 (Washington, D.C.: U.S. Government Printing Of-

fice, 1975); and "Report to the American Physical Society by the Study Group on Light-Water Reactor Safety," *Reviews of Modern Physics* 47 (Summer 1975): suppl. no. 1.

10. See "Source Terms: The New Reactor Safety Debate," *Science News* 127 (1985): 250–53.

11. See, for example, Rae Goodell, "Scientists and the Press: The Case of Recombinant DNA," paper presented at the annual meeting of the American Association for the Advancement of Science, January 1980, 9; E. Wehr, "DNA Regulation Bill Hits Roadblock Again," *Congressional Quarterly Weekly Report*, May 27, 1978, 1331–35.

12. A muted version of the argument that scientists presented a unified front on rDNA research is offered in Sheldon Krimsky, *Genetic Alchemy: The Social History of the Recombinant DNA Controversy* (Cambridge: MIT Press, 1982).

13. For a summary of the NIH guidelines, see U.S. Congress, Office of Technology Assessment, *Impacts of Applied Genetics* (Washington, D.C.: U.S. Government Printing Office, 1981), chapter 11.

14. Not all scientists agreed that biological containment would be entirely effective.

15. List adapted from Sheldon Krimsky, *Genetic Alchemy*, Appendix C, 372–76. This is only an illustrative list of rDNA concerns; it omits significant nonworkshop contributions (such as the July 1974 Berg letter), and it does not report the precise scientific issues (such as the Ascot Workshop's concern about cloning of DNA copies of viroids).

16. Working Group on Revision of the Guidelines, "Evaluation of the Risks Associated with Recombinant DNA Research," *Recombinant DNA Technical Bulletin*, vol. 4 (Washington, D.C.: U.S. Department of Health and Human Services, December 1981), 178; V. W. Franco, "Ethics of Recombinant DNA Research and Technology," *New York State Journal of Medicine* 81 (June 1981): 1039.

17. S. L. Gorbach, letter to Donald Fredrickson, July 14, 1977, reprinted in National Institutes of Health, *Environmental Impact Statement on NIH Guidelines for Research Involving Recombinant DNA Molecules*, Part 2, October 1977, Appendix M: "Issues" (Washington, D.C.: U.S. Government Printing Office, 1980), 25.

18. Sherwood L. Gorbach, "Recombinant DNA: An Infectious Disease Perspective," *Journal of Infectious Diseases* 137 (1978): 615–23; quote from p. 62.

19. S. B. Levy and B. Marshall, "Survival of *E. coli* Host-Vector Systems in the Human Intestinal Tract," *Recombinant DNA Technical Bulletin* 2 (July 1979): 77–80, describes an experiment in which a

common manipulation rendered the enfeebled X1776 strain of *E. coli* K-12 more able to colonize the human intestinal tract. P. S. Cohen et al., "Fecal *E. coli* Strains in the Mouse GI Tract," *Recombinant DNA Technical Bulletin* 2 (November 1979): 106–13, reported on the increased susceptibility under antibiotic treatment.

20. Gorbach, "Recombinant DNA."

21. Working Group on Revision of the Guidelines, 171, 178.

22. W. A. Thomasson, "Recombinant DNA and Regulating Uncertainty," *The Bulletin of the Atomic Scientists* 35 (December 1979): 26–32; quote from 27–28.

23. See MIT biology professors Jonathan King and Ethen Signer, letter to the editor, *The New York Times*, May 3, 1979, which read in part: "At least one application of the recombinant DNA technology results in the creation of a laboratory hybrid not found in nature which does represent a new source of infection. . . . Neither the public nor the scientific community is served when a positive result indicating a danger is buried in a mass of negative data and ignored. Such a situation is truly a hazard to us all."

24. See Barbara Rosenberg and Lee Simon, "Recombinant DNA: Have Recent Experiments Assessed All the Risks?," *Nature* 282 (December 1979): 773–74.

25. U.S. Congress, Subcommittee on Science, Research, and Technology of the Committee on Science and Technology, *Genetic Engineering, Human Genetics,* and *Cell Biology—Evolution of the Technical Issues,* 96th Cong., 2d sess. (Washington, D.C.: U.S. Government Printing Office, 1980), 26.

26. Working Group on Revision of the Guidelines, 172.

27. Ibid., 173.

28. U.S. Congress, Subcommittee on Science, Research, and Technology, 26.

29. Among many other sources on genetic technologies and their social implications, see Robert H. Blank, *The Political Implications of Human Genetic Technology* (Boulder, Colo.: Westview Press, 1981); Office of Technology Assessment, *Genetic Technologies: A New Frontier* (Boulder, Colo.: Westview Press, 1982); and Barbara J. Culliton, "New Biotech Review Board Planned," *Science* 229 (1985): 736–37.

5. Threats to the Ozone Layer

1. The stratosphere begins at an altitude of approximately seven miles and gives way to the ionosphere which is about twenty-five miles above the earth.

2. "Boeing Scientist Alters SST View," *The New York Times,* August 27, 1970, 19.

3. Ibid. Also see Halstead Harrison, "Stratospheric Ozone with Added Water Vapor: Influence of High-Altitude Aircraft," *Science* 170 (1970): 734–36.

4. Study of Critical Environmental Problems (SCEP), *Man's Impact on the Global Environment: Assessment and Recommendations for Action* (Cambridge: MIT Press, 1970), 16.

5. Compare the relatively sensational claims in *The New York Times,* May 18, 1971, 78, with H. S. Johnston, "Reduction of Stratospheric Ozone by Nitrogen Oxide Catalysts from Supersonic Transport Exhaust," *Science* 173 (1971): 517–22.

6. "Making a Case: Theory That Aerosols Deplete Ozone Shield Is Attracting Support," *Wall Street Journal,* December 3, 1975, 1, 27. (Cited hereafter as WSJ, 1975.)

7. Ibid.

8. M. J. Molina and F. S. Rowland, "Stratospheric Sink for Chlorofluoromethanes: Chlorine Atom Catalysed Destruction of Ozone," *Nature* 249 (1974): 810–12. For further detail, see F. S. Rowland and M. J. Molina, "Chlorofluoromethanes in the Environment," *Review of Geophysics and Space Physics* 13 (1975): 1–35.

9. The full process proposed by the chemists was complex, but the essential reaction involves chlorine and ozone reacting to produce oxygen and chlorine oxide: $Cl + O_3 \rightarrow O_2 + ClO$.

10. WSJ, 1975, 1.

11. Ibid.

12. Ibid.

13. Statement of the Jet Propulsion Laboratory atmospheric physicist Crofton B. Farmer, quoted in WSJ, 1975, 27.

14. For example, a number of scientists engaged in direct stratospheric measurements of chlorine oxide, which is one of the short-lived, intermediate products of the chemical sequence hypothesized by Molina and Rowland. See E. M. Weinstock, M. J. Phillips, and J. G. Anderson, "In-Situ Observations of ClO in the Stratosphere: A Review of Recent Results," *Journal of Geophysical Research* 86 (1981): 7273–78.

15. Atmospheric chemist James P. Lodge, Jr., quoted in WSJ, 1975, 1.

16. Ibid., 27.

17. Jeffrey A. Tannenbaum, "Fluorocarbon Battle Expected to Heat Up as the Regulators Move Beyond Aerosols," *Wall Street Journal,* January 19, 1978, 38.

18. Ibid.

19. Federal Task Force on Inadvertent Modification of the Stratosphere, Council on Environmental Quality, Federal Council for Science and Technology, *Fluorocarbons and the Environment* (Washington, D.C.: U.S. Government Printing Office, 1975).

20. A. D. Little & Co., *Preliminary Economic Impact Assessment of Possible Regulatory Action to Control Atmospheric Emissions of Selected Halocarbons* (Washington, D.C.: U.S. Environmental Protection Agency, 1975).

21. Panel on Atmospheric Chemistry of the Committee on Impacts of Stratospheric Change, National Research Council, *Halocarbons: Effects on Stratospheric Ozone* (Washington, D.C.: National Academy of Sciences, 1976).

22. The National Research Council studies not cited elsewhere in this chapter have included: *Environmental Impact of Stratospheric Flight: Biological and Climatic Effects of Aircraft Emissions in the Stratosphere*, 1975; *Halocarbons: Environmental Effects of Chlorofluormethane Release*, 1976; *Protection Against Depletion of Stratospheric Ozone by Chlorofluorocarbons*, 1979. All are published by the National Academy Press, Washington, D.C.

23. Formally sponsored governmental or United Nations studies outside the United States include, among many others: R. D. Hudson et al., eds., *The Stratosphere 1981: Theory and Measurements*, WMO Global Research and Monitoring Project Report no. 11 (Geneva: World Meteorological Organization, 1982); and A. C. Aiken, ed., *Proceedings of the NATO Advanced Study Institute on Atmospheric Ozone: Its Variation and Human Influences* (Washington, D.C.: Federal Aviation Administration, 1980).

24. See U.S. Congress, House of Representatives, *Fluorocarbons—Impact on Health and Environment, Hearings Before the Subcommittee on Public Health and Foreign Commerce on H.R. 17577 and 17545*, 93rd Cong., 2d sess., 1974.

25. Editorial: "The Dilemma of the Endangered Ozone," *The New York Times*, October 29, 1980, A30.

26. "45 Countries Adopt a Treaty to Safeguard Layer of Ozone," *The New York Times*, March 23, 1985, 4; and "U.S. and Common Market Take Opposite Sides in Ozone Dispute," *Christian Science Monitor*," January 31, 1985, 14.

27. P. J. Crutzen, "Estimates of Possible Variations in Total Ozone Due to Natural Causes and Human Activities," *Ambio* 3 (1974): 201-10.

28. P. J. Crutzen, "Upper Limits in Atmospheric Ozone Reductions Following Increased Application of Fixed Nitrogen to the Soil," *Geophysical Research Letter*, 3 (1976): 169-72.

29. For example, see S. C. Liu et al., "Limitation of Fertilizer Induced Ozone Reduction by the Long Lifetime of the Reservoir of Fixed Nitrogen," *Geophysical Research Letter* 3 (1976): 157–60.

30. Harold S. Johnston, "Analysis of the Independent Variables in the Perturbation of Stratospheric Ozone by Nitrogen Fertilizers," *Journal of Geophysical Research* 82 (1977): 1767–72.

31. National Academy of Sciences/National Research Council, *Nitrates: An Environmental Assessment* (Washington, D.C.: National Academy Press, 1978).

32. S. Fred Singer, "Stratospheric Water Vapour Increase Due to Human Activities," *Nature* 233 (1971): 543–45.

33. P. R. Zimmerman, J. P. Greenberg, S. O. Wandiga, and P. J. Crutzen, "Termites: A Potentially Large Source of Atmospheric Methane, Carbon Dioxide, and Molecular Hydrogen," *Science* 218 (1982): 563–65.

34. National Research Council, *Stratospheric Ozone Depletion by Halocarbons: Chemistry and Transport* (Washington, D.C.: National Academy Press, 1979).

35. V. Ramanathan, R. J. Cicerone, H. B. Singh, and J. T. Kiehl, "Trace Gas Trends and Their Potential Role in Climate Change," *Journal of Geophysical Research* 90 (1985): 5547–66.

36. Michael J. Prather, Michael B. McElroy, and Steven C. Wofsy, "Reductions in Ozone at High Concentrations of Stratospheric Halogens," *Nature* 312 (1984): 227–31.

37. National Research Council, *Stratospheric Ozone Depletion by Halocarbons*.

38. National Research Council, *Causes and Effects of Stratospheric Ozone Reduction: An Update* (Washington, D.C.: National Academy Press, 1982). The original research is reported in R. D. Hudson et al., *The Stratosphere 1981: Theory and Measurements*, WMO Global Research and Monitoring Project Report no. 11 (Geneva: World Meteorological Organization, 1982).

39. National Research Council, *Causes and Effects*, 29.

40. National Research Council, *Causes and Effects of Changes in Stratospheric Ozone Depletion: Update 1983* (Washington, D.C.: National Academy Press, 1984).

41. Prather et al., "Reductions in Ozone."

42. Boyce Rensberger, "EPA Finds Greater Peril to Earth's Ozone Shield," *Washington Post,* April 5, 1985, A4.

43. Philip Shabecoff, "Suit Is Filed to Bar Possible Harm to Earth's Protective Ozone Layer," *The New York Times,* November 28, 1984, A20.

44. National Research Council, *Causes and Effects . . . Update 1983*, 12.

45. A related idea for limiting the magnitude of error is the proposal that the government auction off the right to extract a fixed amount of scarce natural resources each year. Such action would not prevent depletion problems but would ameliorate them. See Herman E. Daly, *The Steady-State Economy* (San Francisco: W. H. Freeman, 1977).

46. EPA Assistant Administrator for Toxic Substances Steven Jellinek, quoted in *The New York Times,* October 8, 1980, A18.

6. The Greenhouse Threat

1. Roger Revelle and Walter Munk, "The Carbon Dioxide Cycle and the Biosphere," in National Research Council, *Energy and Climate* (Washington, D.C.: National Academy of Sciences, 1977), 140–58.

2. V. Ramanathan et al., "Trace Gas Trends and Their Potential Role in Climate Change."

3. Carbon Dioxide Assessment Committee, National Research Council, *Changing Climate* (Washington, D.C.: National Academy Press, 1983), 135, 138.

4. Among other sources, see Syukuro Manabe and Richard T. Wetherald, "On the Distribution of Climate Change Resulting from an Increase in CO_2 Content of the Atmosphere," *Journal of the Atmospheric Sciences* 37 (1980): 99–118.

5. On the ramifications, see Charles F. Cooper, "What Might Man-Induced Climate Change Mean?," *Foreign Affairs* 56 (1978): 500–520; Walter Orr Roberts, "It Is Time to Prepare for Global Climate Changes," *Conservation Foundation Letter,* April 1983; William W. Kellogg and Robert Schware, *Climate Change and Societal Consequences of Increasing Atmospheric Carbon Dioxide* (Boulder, Colo.: Westview Press, 1981); and Hermann Flohn, *Life on a Warmer Earth: Possible Climatic Consequences of Man-Made Global Warming* (Laxenburg, Austria: International Institute for Applied Systems Analysis, 1981).

6. J. Hansen, D. Johnson, A. Lacis, S. Lebedeff, P. Lee, D. Rind, and G. Russell, "Climate Impact of Increasing Atmospheric Carbon Dioxide," *Science* 213 (1981): 957–66; quote from 965.

7. For additional discussion and calculations, see John S. Hoffman, Dale Keyes, and James G. Titus, *Projecting Future Sea Level Rise: Methodology, Estimates to the Year 2100, and Research Needs,*

2nd ed., rev. (Washington, D.C.: Office of Policy and Resources Management, U.S. Environmental Protection Agency, October 24, 1983). For an example of the impact on a specific coastal city, see U.S. Environmental Protection Agency, *The Effects and Value of Sea Level Rise on Charleston and Galveston* (Washington, D.C.: EPA, 1983).

8. Council on Environmental Quality, *Global Energy Futures and the Carbon Dioxide Problem* (Washington, D.C.: Council on Environmental Quality, January 1981), p. 29.

9. J. Tyndall, "On Radiation Through the Earth's Atmosphere," *Philosophical Magazine* 4 (1863): 200.

10. Svante Arrhenius, "On the Influence of Carbonic Acid in the Air Upon the Temperature of the Ground," *Philosophical Magazine* 41 (1896): 237–76.

11. T. C. Chamberlin, "An Attempt to Frame a Working Hypothesis of the Cause of Glacial Periods on an Atmospheric Basis," *Journal of Geology* 7 (1899): 545–84, 667–85, 751–87.

12. G. S. Callendar, "The Artificial Production of Carbon Dioxide and Its Influence on Temperature," *Quarterly Journal of the Royal Meteorological Society* 64 (1938): 223–40; and "Can Carbon Dioxide Influence Climate?" *Weather* 4 (1949): 310–14.

13. Gilbert N. Plass, "The Carbon Dioxide Theory of Climate Change," *Tellus* 8 (1956): 140–54.

14. Roger Revelle and Hans E. Suess, "Carbon Dioxide Exchange Between Atmosphere and Ocean and the Question of an Increase of Atmospheric CO$_2$ During the Past Decades," *Tellus* 9 (1957): 18–27.

15. The Conservation Foundation, *Implications of Rising Carbon Dioxide Content of the Atmosphere* (New York: Conservation Foundation, 1963).

16. President's Science Advisory Committee, Environmental Pollution Panel, *Restoring the Quality of Our Environment* (Washington, D.C.: The White House, 1965), Appendix Y4, 112–33.

17. SCEP, *Man's Impact on the Global Environment.*

18. Study of Man's Impact on Climate (SMIC), *Inadvertent Climate Modification* (Cambridge: MIT Press, 1971).

19. U.S. Committee for the Global Atmospheric Research Program, *Understanding Climatic Change: A Program for Action* (Washington, D.C.: National Academy of Sciences, 1975); Joint Organizing Committee, *The Physical Basis of Climate and Climate Modelling,* (Geneva: Joint Planning Staff, Global Atmospheric Research Programme, 1975).

20. B. Bolin, E. T. Degens, S. Kempe, and P. Ketner, eds., *The Global Carbon Cycle,* Proceedings of a SCOPE Workshop, Ratzeburg, German Federal Republic, March 21–26, 1977 (New York: Wiley, 1979); W. Stumm, ed., *Global Chemical Cycles and Their Alterations by Man,* Proceedings of the Dahlem Workshop, November 15–19, 1976 (Berlin: Berlin Abakon Verlagsgesellschaft, 1977).

21. Reported in Peter David, "Two Views on Whether More Means Doom," *Nature* 305 (October 27, 1983): 751.

An example of the type of research being funded is an effort to use satellites to measure changes in global forestation and their carbon content; see G. M. Woodwell et al., *Deforestation Measured by LANDSAT: Steps Toward a Method,* prepared for the Carbon Dioxide Research Division, Department of Energy (New York: Brookhaven National Laboratory, 1983).

22. See, for example, Senate Governmental Affairs Committee, *Carbon Dioxide Accumulation in the Atmosphere, Synthetic Fuels, and Energy Policy: A Symposium,* 96th Cong., 1st sess., 1979.

23. A. Lacis, J. Hansen, P. Lee, T. Mitchell, and S. Lebedeff, "Greenhouse Effect of Trace Gases, 1970–80," *Geophysical Research Letters* 8 (1981): 1035–38. For similar conclusions, see V. Ramanathan, "Climatic Effects of Anthropogenic Trace Gases," in Wilfrid Bach, J. Pankrath, and J. Williams, eds., *Interactions of Energy and Climate* (Hingham, Mass.: D. Reidel, 1980), 269–80; J. Chamberlain, H. Foley, G. MacDonald, and M. Ruderman, "Climate Effects of Minor Atmospheric Constituents," in William C. Clark, ed., *Carbon Dioxide Review 1982* (New York: Oxford University Press, 1982); and Gordon J. MacDonald, ed., *The Long-Term Impacts of Increasing Atmospheric Carbon Dioxide Levels* (Cambridge: Ballinger, 1982), 113–26.

24. Richard C. J. Somerville, Scripps Institute of Oceanography, paper delivered at the meeting of the American Geophysical Union, San Francisco, December 1984, quoted in Robert C. Cowen, "New CO_2 Data Undercuts Dire Prediction Icecaps Would Melt," *Christian Science Monitor,* December 12, 1984, 29, 31; quote from 29.

25. David E. Lincoln, Nasser Sionit, and Boyd R. Strain, paper delivered at the meeting of the American Geophysical Union, San Francisco, December 1984, quoted in ibid.

On stream runoff, see S. B. Idso and A. J. Brazel, "Rising Atmospheric Carbon Dioxide Concentrations May Increase Stream Flow," *Nature* 312 (1984): 51–53.

26. An early view expressing concern about deforestation was B. Bolin, "Changes of Land Biota and Their Importance for the Carbon

Cycle," *Science* 196 (1977): 613–15; the mainstream view was advanced in W. S. Broecker et al., "Fate of Fossil Fuel Carbon Dioxide and the Global Budget," *Science* 206 (1979): 409–18.

A more recent statement of the dispute is in NRC, *Changing Climate:* compare the "Synthesis" by the full committee, especially 16–21, with the view of committee member George M. Woodwell, "Biotic Effects on the Concentration of Atmospheric Carbon Dioxide: A Review and Projection," 216–41.

27. Lacis et al., "Greenhouse Effect of Trace Gases." Also see L. Donner and V. Ramanathan, "Methane and Nitrous Oxide: Their Effects on Terrestrial Climate," *Journal of the Atmospheric Sciences* 37 (1980): 119–24.

28. On this point, see P. R. Bell, "Methane Hydrate and the Carbon Dioxide Question," in Clark, *Carbon Dioxide Review;* Roger R. Revelle, "Methane Hydrates in Continental Slope Sediments and Increasing Atmospheric Carbon Dioxide," in NRC, *Changing Climate,* 252–61.

29. Wei-Chyung Wang, Joseph P. Pinto, and Yuk Ling Yung, "Climatic Effects Due to Halogenated Compounds in the Earth's Atmosphere," *Journal of the Atmospheric Sciences* 37 (1980): 333–38.

30. Ramanathan et al., "Trace Gas Trends," 5562.

31. William A. Nierenberg, quoted in James Gleick, "Rare Gases May Speed the Warming of the Earth," *The New York Times,* April 30, 1985, C1–C2; quote from C1.

32. Compare Hansen et al., "Climate Impact," with Roger Revelle, "Carbon Dioxide and World Climate," *Scientific American* 247 (August 1982): 35–43. The reassuring research relies on historical geological evidence, the alarming, on mathematical climate modeling.

33. The NRC had recently issued Climate Research Board, *Carbon Dioxide and Climate: A Scientific Assessment* (Washington, D.C.: National Academy of Sciences, 1979).

34. Energy Security Act of 1980, Public Law 96-294, June 30, 1980; 42 USC 8911, Title VII—Acid Precipitation Program and Carbon Dioxide Study; Subtitle B—Carbon Dioxide.

35. NRC, *Changing Climate;* and a companion volume, NRC, *CO2 and Climate: A Second Assessment* (Washington, D.C.: National Academy Press, 1982).

36. NRC, *Changing Climate,* 26.

37. Ramanathan et al., "Trace Gas Trends," especially, 5557, 5559.

38. NRC, *Changing Climate,* 64.

39. For example, see W. Hafele et al., *Energy in a Finite World:*

A Global Systems Analysis, 2 vols. (Laxenburg, Austria: International Institute for Applied Systems Analysis, 1981).

40. Walter Sullivan, "Report Urges Steps to Slow Down Climate Warming," *The New York Times,* January 3, 1984, C5.

41. On the flaws in recent projections and the problems likely to be encountered in the future, see U.S. Department of Energy, Office of Policy, Planning, and Analysis, *Energy Projections to the Year 2010* (Washington, D.C.: U.S. Government Printing Office, October 1983).

42. Adapted from Stephen Seidel and Dale Keyes, *Can We Delay a Greenhouse Warming?* (Washington, D.C.: U.S. Environmental Protection Agency, September 1983), 4/27. (Cited hereafter as *Greenhouse Warming.*)

43. In addition to the previously cited sources on the weaknesses of energy forecasting, see William L. Ascher, *Forecasting: An Appraisal for Policy Makers and Planners* (Baltimore, Md.: Johns Hopkins University Press, 1978).

44. For details on the IEA/EPA model, see Jae Edmonds and John Reilly, "A Long-Term Global Energy-Economic Model of Carbon Dioxide Release from Fossil Fuel Use," *Energy Economics* 5 (1983): 74–88.

45. Seidel and Keyes, *Greenhouse Warming,* 4/28–4/32.

46. Ibid., 4/33–4/41.

47. The original suggestion was from Cesare Marchetti, "On Geoengineering and the CO_2 Problem," *Climatic Change* 1 (1977): 59–68. Significant doubts are expressed in A. Albanese and M. Steinberg, *Environmental Control Technology for Atmospheric Carbon Dioxide,* prepared for the U.S. Department of Energy (New York: Brookhaven National Laboratory, 1980). A more hopeful view is in Philip H. Abelson, Editorial: "Carbon Dioxide Emissions," *Science* 222 (1983): 1228.

48. The first extended discussion of the idea apparently was by Freeman Dyson, "Can We Control the Amount of Carbon Dioxide in the Atmosphere?," (unpublished manuscript, Institute for Energy Analysis, Oak Ridge, Tennessee, 1976).

49. D. Greenberg, "Sequestering" (unpublished manuscript prepared for the Office of Policy Analysis, U.S. Environmental Protection Agency, Washington, D.C., 1982); and Gordon J. MacDonald, ed., *The Long-Term Impacts of Increasing Atmospheric Carbon Dioxide Levels* (Cambridge: Ballinger, 1982).

50. Seidel and Keyes, *Greenhouse Warming,* 6/10–6/12. The origi-

nal calculations are in J. Brewbaker, ed., "Giant Leucaena (Koa Haole) Energy Tree Farm" (Hawaii Natural Energy Institute, 1980).

51. Seidel and Keyes, *Greenhouse Warming,* 6/13.

52. The concept of injecting sulfur dioxide into the atmosphere is reviewed briefly in ibid., 6/13–6/14, and in greater detail in W. S. Broeker, J. H. Nuckolls, P. S. Connell, and J. Chang, "SO_2: Backstop Against a Bad CO_2 Trip?" (unpublished manuscript, 1983).

53. See, for example, Lester B. Lave, "A More Feasible Social Response," *Technology Review* 84 (November–December 1981): 23, 28–31.

54. Roberts, "Global Climate Changes," 8.

55. Recent research on ice core samples has suggested that preindustrial carbon dioxide levels were at the extreme low end of those generally believed credible. See D. Raymond and J. M. Barnola, "An Antarctic Ice Core Reveals Atmospheric CO_2 Variations Over the Past Few Centuries," *Nature* 315 (1985): 309–11.

56. Compare Climate Research Board, 1979; with NRC, *CO_2 and Climate;* Revelle, "Carbon Dioxide"; NRC, *Changing Climate;* and Seidel and Keyes, *Greenhouse Warming.*

57. Don G. Scroggin and Robert H. Harris, "Reduction at the Source," *Technology Review* 84 (November–December 1981): 22, 24–28; quote from 26–27. Because the issue of concern is the total level of CO_2 in the atmosphere, stabilization at a given level can be achieved either by high releases for a short period or lower releases for a longer period. The latter obviously is the conservative option.

58. NRC, *Changing Climate,* 65.

59. J. Hansen, G. Russell, A. Lacis, I. Fung, D. Rind, and P. Stone, "Climate Response Times: Dependence on Climate Sensitivity and Ocean Mixing," *Science* 229 (1985): 857–859; quote from 857.

7. A System for Averting Catastrophe

1. Todd R. LaPorte, "On the Design and Management of Nearly Error-Free Organizational Control Systems," in David L. Sills et al., eds., *Accident at Three Mile Island: The Human Dimensions* (Boulder, Colo: Westview Press, 1982), 185–200.

2. Strictly speaking, containment can never be 100 percent certain; it is a matter of degree. Relevant experts can be more or less confident that containment will hold—but never absolutely sure. For small reactors and most rDNA experiments, most members of the relevant scientific community were very confident about containment.

3. "Test Wrecks Reactor, Delights Researchers," *Science* 229 (1985): 538.

4. Aaron Wildavsky, "The Assessment of Safety Goals and Achievements in Complex Technological Systems: The Integration of Technological and Institutional Considerations" (unpublished manuscript prepared for the U.S. Nuclear Regulatory Commission, September 1983), 84.

5. See, for example, any issue of the journal *Risk Analysis*.

6. In his early works, Simon referred to the analytic approach variously as the classical, economic, or objectively rational approach to decision making; Lindblom called it the synoptic, root-and-branch, or analytic approach. See Herbert A. Simon, *Administrative Behavior* (New York: Macmillan, 1947, 1957); "A Behavioral Model of Rational Choice," *Quarterly Journal of Economics* 69 (1955): 99–118; and (with James March) *Organizations* (New York: Wiley, 1958). See Charles E. Lindblom, "The Science of Muddling Through," *Public Administration Review* 19 (1959): 79–88; and (with David Braybrooke) *A Strategy of Decision* (New York: Free Press, 1963). Also see John D. Steinbruner, *The Cybernetic Theory of Decision* (Princeton: Princeton University Press, 1974) for an excellent review and critique of what he calls "the analytic paradigm."

7. $EV = P_1V_1 + P_2V_2 \ldots + P_nV_n$, where "EV" is the expected value of a given alternative, each numerical subscript refers to one of the consequences of the alternative, "P" to probability, and "V" to value.

8. There are many applications of the analytic strategy: decision tree, cost-benefit, and risk-benefit analyses are prominent examples. There are also many variations in the strategy itself. The utility maximization decision rule is, under certain conditions, replaced by minimax or maximin. The exhaustive search, in some variations, is limited to feasible alternatives. In other variations, where alternatives are simply assumed to be available, search is not a part of the process. Finally, the requirement that the likelihoods of consequences be estimated is frequently modified to require that subjective estimates of likelihoods be made and then revised as information becomes available.

9. In addition to the works already cited, see Amitai Etzioni, *Social Problems* (Englewood Cliffs, N.J.: Prentice-Hall, 1976); and Yzekiel Dror, *Ventures in Policy Sciences* (New York: American Elsevier, 1971).

10. For further discussion of this point, see the criticisms of the Rasmussen Report on reactor safety by an American Physical Society

study group in "Report to the APS by the Study Group on Light Water Reactor Safety," *Reviews of Modern Physics* 47 (1975): suppl. no. 1.

11. See, for example, U.S. General Accounting Office, *Probabilistic Risk Assessment: An Emerging Aid to Nuclear Power Plant Safety Regulation* (Washington, D.C.: U.S. General Accounting Office, June 19, 1985).

12. Other observers have been coming to similar conclusions. For example, Schmandt has noted that "regulatory science has not yet helped in setting priorities and rationalizing agency actions." He wants it to become "a tool for selecting and focusing on the most serious health and environmental dangers." See Jurgen Schmandt, "Regulation and Science," *Science, Technology and Human Values* 9 (1984): 23–38; quote from 33–34.

For a related view, see Giandomenico Majone, "Science and Trans-Science in Standard Setting," *Science, Technology, and Human Values* 9 (1984): 15–21.

13. There has been some attention to variations in the institutional settings within which decisions are made. Lindblom's strategy, for example, is adapted to pluralistic, fragmented arenas. March and Simon's is intended for formal organizations in general, Steinbruner's for formal government organizations, and Cyert and March's for business organizations. Different institutions tend to tackle somewhat different types of problems, of course, but the correspondence is very loose.

14. A well-known example is the case of changes in Connecticut traffic laws that "caused" a spurious drop in accidents. See Donald T. Campbell, "Reforms as Experiments," *American Psychologist* 24 (1969): 409–20.

15. Todd R. LaPorte, ed., *Organized Social Complexity* (Princeton: Princeton University Press, 1975).

A good statement of the presumption about decomposability is in Herbert A. Simon, "The Architecture of Complexity," *General Systems Yearbook* 10 (1975): 63–76.

16. For risky technologies, problematic causal links are less of a problem than is the potential for catastrophe. If the severe consequences were to emerge, we would have a pretty fair idea of what caused them. Unclear causal links do complicate some of the issues, of course—such as the difficulty of linking observed temperature changes to CO_2 emissions or of tracing a health effect to a particular chemical.

17. Aaron Wildavsky, *Speaking Truth to Power* (Boston, Mass.: Little, Brown, 1979).

18. On the difficulties of quasi-experiments, see Walter Williams and Richard F. Elmore, *Studying Implementation: Methodological and Administrative Issues* (Chatham, N.J.: Chatham House Publishers, 1982).

19. See, for example, Graham T. Allison, *Essence of Decision: Explaining the Cuban Missile Crisis* (Boston, Mass.: Little, Brown, 1971).

20. Irving L. Janis and Leon Mann, *Decision Making: a Psychological Analysis of Conflict, Choice, and Commitment* (New York: Free Press, 1977).

21. For another effort to characterize decision problems, see David Braybrooke and Charles E. Lindblom, *A Strategy of Decision* (New York: Free Press, 1963), 78.

22. A handful of other attempts have been made to think systematically about the structure of political problems and the need to match problem and strategy, including Ian Lustick, "Explaining the Variable Utility of Disjointed Incrementalism: Four Propositions," *American Political Science Review* 74 (1980), 342–53; Paul R. Schulman, *Large-Scale Policy Making* (New York: American Elsevier, 1980); and Robert Goodin and Ilmar Waldner, "Thinking Big, Thinking Small, and Not Thinking at All," *Public Policy* 27 (1979): 1–24.

8. Can We Do Better?

1. On the recent criticisms, see Marjorie Sun, "Food Dyes Fuel Debate Over Delaney," *Science* 229 (1985): 739–41.

2. There is a large and growing literature on the subject of acceptable risk. An early statement was William W. Lowrance's, *Of Acceptable Risk: Science and the Determination of Safety* (Los Altos, Calif.: William Kaufman, 1976); a recent overview is William W. Lowrance's, *Modern Science and Human Values* (New York: Oxford University Press, 1985). Also see Richard C. Schwing and Walter A. Albers, *Societal Risk Assessment: How Safe Is Safe Enough?* (New York: Plenum, 1980).

3. See, for example, A. V. Cohen and D. K. Pritchard, *Comparative Risks of Electricity Production Systems: A Critical Survey of the Literature,* Health and Safety Executive, Research Paper no. 11 (London: Her Majesty's Stationery Office, 1980).

4. U.S. Nuclear Regulatory Commission, *Safety Goal for Nuclear Power Plants: A Discussion Paper* (Washington, D.C.: U.S. Nuclear Regulatory Commission, 1982).

5. Ibid., xi.

6. 5/10,000   ×   0.1% ×   200 persons   =   1/10,000

(overall	(acceptable	(population	(annual probability
accident	reactor	near	of one death from
death rate)	death rate)	reactor)	reactor accident)

7. For a discussion of the uncertainty and associated controversy surrounding the size of the source term—the amount of fission products that escape in a serious accident—see "Source Terms: The New Reactor Safety Debate," *Science News* 127 (1984): 250–53.

8. For a typical example, see Edmund A. C. Crouch and Richard Wilson, *Risk/Benefit Analysis* (Cambridge: Ballinger, 1982).

9. J. G. U. Adams, ". . . And How Much for Your Grandmother?," reprinted in Steven E. Rhoads, ed., *Valuing Life: Public Policy Dilemmas* (Boulder, Colo.: Westview Press, 1980), 135–46.

10. Anthony V. Nero, Jr., "The Indoor Radon Story," *Technology Review* 89 (January 1986): 28–40.

11. This example is adapted from Table 6, p. 534, in E. P O'Donnell and J. J. Mauro, "A Cost-Benefit Comparison of Nuclear and Nonnuclear Health and Safety Protective Measures and Regulations," *Nuclear Safety* 20 (1979): 525–40. For a different analysis that makes the same basic point, see Crouch and Wilson, *Risk/Benefit Analysis*.

12. See, for example, the brief reference in NRC, *Changing Climate,* 4.

13. Alvin M. Weinberg and Irving Spiewak, "Inherently Safe Reactors and a Second Nuclear Era," *Science* 224 (1984): 1398–1402.

14. See *NRDC* v. *Train*, 8 ERC 2120 (D.D.C. 1976) and *NRDC* v. *Costle*, 12 ERC 1830 (D.D.C. 1979).

15. For a more extended analysis of this issue, see Giandomenico Majone, "Science and Trans-Science in Standard Setting."

16. NRC, *Changing Climate*, 3.

17. President's Commission on the Accident at Three Mile Island, *The Need for Change: The Legacy of TMI* (Washington, D.C.: U.S. Government Printing Office, October 1979), 56.

18. Alvin M. Weinberg et al., "The Second Nuclear Era," research memorandum ORAU/IEA-84-(M) (Oak Ridge, Tenn.: Institute for Energy Analysis, February 1984), 57.

19. And there are other methods to promote learning. For example, one possible benefit of "energy parks," with a number of reactors close together, is that learning could occur via informal contacts among personnel; see Alvin M. Weinberg, "Nuclear Safety and Public Acceptance," presented at the International ENS/ANS Con-

Cycles, Brussels, April 30, 1982.

20. On the Bhopal incident, see the special issue of *Chemical and Engineering News* 63 (February 11, 1985), and the investigative reports in *The New York Times,* January 28 through February 3, 1985.

21. Stuart Diamond, "Carbide Asserts String of Errors Caused Gas Leak," *The New York Times,* August 24, 1985, 1.

22. For an overview of chemical plant safety issues, see Charles Perrow, *Normal Accidents* (New York: Basic Books, 1984), 101–22.

23. Lewis Mumford, *The Pentagon of Power* (New York: Harcourt Brace Jovanovich, 1970), 410.

24. Jacques Ellul, *The Technological System* (New York: Continuum, 1980), 117.

25. Albert Schweitzer, quoted in Rachel Carson, *Silent Spring* (Boston, Mass.: Houghton Mifflin, 1962), v.

Index

Acid rain, and greenhouse strategy, 109
Agriculture: and pesticide dangers to workers, 179n.13; and pests, effects of climate on, 107; and plant growth, effects of carbon dioxide on, 107; and precipitation patterns, possible shift in, 99; and water shortages, 113–114
Air pollution strategy, 109
Air traffic control, 125; and crisis decision making, 147
Alkyltins, 31
Alliance for Responsible CFC Policy, 83
Allied Chemical, 20
American Chemical Society, 82
American Physical Society, 63
Analytic approach: in decision theory, 137, 140; examples of, 198n.8; and expected value approach, limitations of, 137; and safety goal, 160; in support of strategy, 140; and targeted R&D, 168; variations in, 198n.8
Argonne National Lab, 37, 39
Arrhenius, Svante, 101
Arsenic: accumulation in soils, 16; in persistent pesticides, 15, 20; residue levels, 18–19
Asbestos, 14; delayed feedback on, 4
Ascot, England, conference (1978), 72
Atmospheric threats: and inapplica-

bility of typical strategies, 76; intervention against, tactics for, 112–113. *See also* Climate warming; Fluorocarbons; Fossil fuels; Greenhouse threat; Ozone
Atomic Energy Commission, U.S., 52; and conflict of interest, 64; and earliest reactors, 37–38, 132; and early commercial reactors, 40–41; flaws in decision-making process, 5; and Rasmussen report, 62; and remote siting, deemphasis of, 41–42; and remote test site, 38; revised strategy, 43–44; underlying approach, 45
Attention-cycle, ozone, 94
Ausloos, Peter J., 80
Automobiles, risks of, 154–155

Bacteria. *See* Recombinant DNA research
Bans: on fluorocarbon aerosols, 92; on rDNA experiments, 66; on refrigerant chemicals, 91. *See also* Initial precautions
Bayport, Texas, 19
Bees, effects of pesticides on, 15
Benzidine-based dyes, 31
Berg, Paul, 58
Bhopal accident, 2, 14; description of, 171; as example of egregious risk, 171–172; and Institute, West Virginia, accident, 172

Compositor: Huron Valley Graphics
Text: 10/12 Times Roman
Display: Goudy Bold and Times Roman
Printer: Murray Printing Co.